2ⁿᵈ EDITION

Ventures 3

WORKBOOK

Gretchen Bitterlin   Dennis Johnson   Donna Price   Sylvia Ramirez

K. Lynn Savage (Series Editor)

with Ingrid Wisniewska

 CAMBRIDGE
UNIVERSITY PRESS

CAMBRIDGE
UNIVERSITY PRESS

University Printing House, Cambridge CB2 8BS, United Kingdom

One Liberty Plaza, 20th Floor, New York, NY 10006, USA

477 Williamstown Road, Port Melbourne, VIC 3207, Australia

4843/24, 2nd Floor, Ansari Road, Daryaganj, Delhi – 110002, India

79 Anson Road, #06–04/06, Singapore 079906

Cambridge University Press is part of the University of Cambridge.

It furthers the University's mission by disseminating knowledge in the pursuit of education, learning and research at the highest international levels of excellence.

www.cambridge.org
Information on this title: www.cambridge.org/9781107640016

First published 2008
20 19 18 17 16 15 14 13 12 11 10 9

Printed in Dubai by Oriental Press

A catalogue record for this publication is available from the British Library

ISBN 978-1-107-68472-0 Student's Book with Audio CD
ISBN 978-1-107-64001-6 Workbook with Audio CD
ISBN 978-1-139-88472-3 Online Workbook
ISBN 978-1-107-65217-0 Teacher's Edition with Assessment Audio CD / CD-ROM
ISBN 978-1-107-66076-2 Class Audio CDs
ISBN 978-1-107-64952-1 Presentation Plus

Additional resources for this publication at www.cambridge.org/ventures

Cambridge University Press has no responsibility for the persistence or accuracy of URLs for external or third-party internet websites referred to in this publication, and does not guarantee that any content on such websites is, or will remain, accurate or appropriate.

Art direction, book design, photo research, and layout services: Q2A / Bill Smith
Audio production: CityVox, LLC

Contents

Jose - S.

Welcome

1 **Listen. Then circle the correct answers.**

TRACK 2

1. Right now, Moy is _____.
   a. working for his uncle
   b. starting his own business
   c. studying at Valley Tech

2. Moy's main goal is _____.
   a. to talk to Ms. Hall
   b. to start his own business
   c. to save some money

3. The first step in Moy's plan is _____.
   a. to get a job with his uncle
   b. to pass an exam and get his license
   c. to work hard and save money

4. Last summer, Moy _____.
   a. worked for his uncle
   b. studied at Valley Tech
   c. passed his exam

5. Ms. Hall says that Moy _____.
   a. will have to graduate in June
   b. will need to save money
   c. will start his business right away

6. Moy hopes to have his own business _____.
   a. in about five years
   b. in June
   c. this summer

Check your answers. See page 134.

2 Complete the sentences about Mayra's goal.

Mayra has a degree in nursing from a university in Guatemala. Now she lives in Houston, Texas.

1. Mayra _____*wants to get*_____ a job in a hospital in Houston, Texas.
   (want / get)

2. First, she _____ her English.
   (need / improve)

3. Second, she _____ more nursing classes at a university.
   (need / take)

4. Then she _____ a U.S. nursing license.
   (need / get)

5. Finally, she _____ for jobs at several hospitals.
   (need / apply)

6. Mayra _____ as a nurse because she likes to help people.
   (want / work)

3 Write sentences. Use the information in the chart.

Name	Want to	Need to
Emile	1. open a men's clothing store	2. find a good location for the store
Farah and Ali	3. study engineering in college	4. take a lot of math classes
Monica	5. pass the GED exam	6. take some special classes
Adrian	7. buy a new car	8. save his money

1. Emile *wants to open a men's clothing store.* _____

2. He _____

3. Farah and Ali _____

4. _____

5. Monica _____

6. _____

7. Adrian _____

8. _____

4 Complete the sentences. Use the simple present or the present continuous.

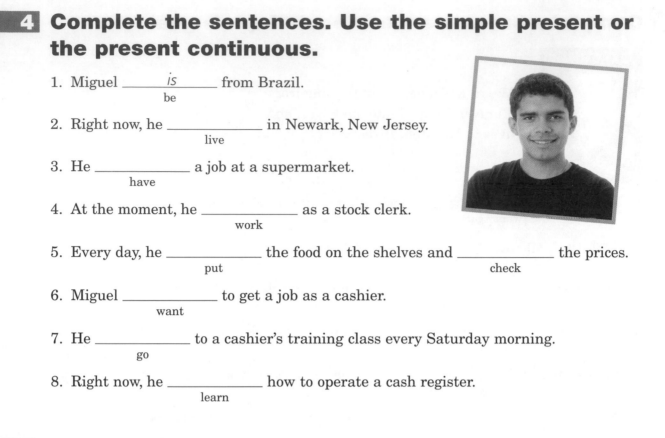

1. Miguel ____is____ from Brazil.
   be

2. Right now, he _____ in Newark, New Jersey.
   live

3. He _____ a job at a supermarket.
   have

4. At the moment, he _____ as a stock clerk.
   work

5. Every day, he _____ the food on the shelves and _____ the prices.
   put   check

6. Miguel _____ to get a job as a cashier.
   want

7. He _____ to a cashier's training class every Saturday morning.
   go

8. Right now, he _____ how to operate a cash register.
   learn

5 Write sentences. Use the simple present or the present continuous.

1. at the moment / Miguel / live / with his brother Tony

   At the moment, Miguel is living with his brother Tony.

2. Tony / have / a job / at a computer store

   _____

3. right now / he / work / as a salesperson

   _____

4. he / want / become / a computer technician

   _____

5. Tony / take / English classes / every Thursday evening

   _____

6. Tony and Miguel / study / English together / now

   _____

Check your answers. See page 134.

6 Complete the sentences. Use the simple past or the future.

1. Michio Tarumi ____came____ to the United States in 2008.
   come

2. At that time, he _____ to become a professional baseball player.
   want

3. He _____ for a team in a small town in Florida for two years.
   play

4. Then he _____ to help some boys in the town form their own baseball team.
   begin

5. After that, Michio _____ to change his career plan.
   decide

6. Next September, Michio _____ a new job at a sports center in the town.
   start

7. Michio _____ working with the boys' baseball team last year.
   like

8. In the future, Michio _____ more young people to play baseball and other sports.
   teach

7 Read the answers. Complete the questions.

1. When _did you come to this country_____?

   I came to this country in 2008.

2. Why _____?

   I came here because I wanted to become a professional baseball player.

3. What team _____?

   I played for a team in a small town in Florida.

4. How long _____?

   I played for them for two years.

5. Why _____?

   I decided to change my career plan because I like working with young people.

6. When _____?

   I'll start my new job with the sports center in September.

7. What _____?

   I'll teach young people to play baseball and other sports.

8. How long _____?

   I'm not sure, but I hope I will stay in this town for a long time.

LESSON **A** Listening

1 **Read and circle the correct answers. Then listen.**

TRACK 3

Juliana

Anika

> Juliana and Anika are friends. Juliana is quiet and shy. She dislikes going to dance clubs or other noisy places. She often writes e-mails to her friends, but she doesn't like meeting new people. She likes being alone or meeting with just one or two friends. On the weekend, she likes staying home. She loves reading and watching movies. Last weekend, she read two books and watched three movies.
>
> Anika is very different from Juliana. She is friendly and outgoing. She dislikes being alone at home. She loves meeting new people and talking on her cell phone. On the weekend, she enjoys dancing and going to parties with a group of her friends. Last night, they went to a dance club and danced until midnight.

1. Juliana dislikes _____.
   a. going out
   b. reading books
   c. writing e-mails
   d. watching movies

2. Juliana likes _____.
   a. meeting people
   b. talking
   c. staying home
   d. dance clubs

3. Juliana isn't _____.
   a. quiet
   b. outgoing
   c. shy
   d. happy

4. Anika dislikes _____.
   a. dancing
   b. dance clubs
   c. staying home
   d. going to parties

5. Anika likes _____.
   a. making friends
   b. staying home
   c. being alone
   d. writing e-mails

6. Anika isn't _____.
   a. outgoing
   b. friendly
   c. shy
   d. fun

Check your answers. See page 134.

2 Complete the sentences. Use the information in Exercise 1.

| alone | dislikes | enjoys | going out | outgoing | shy |

1. Anika is an _____ person.

2. Juliana _____ meeting with only one or two people at a time.

3. Anika likes _____ with her friends.

4. Juliana _____ going to parties.

5. Juliana is quiet and _____ .

6. Anika doesn't like being _____ .

3 Circle the correct word.

1. Pietro is quiet. He **enjoys** / **(dislikes)** talking.

2. Salma is outgoing. She **enjoys** / **dislikes** meeting new people.

3. Chen is friendly. He **enjoys** / **dislikes** talking to other people.

4. Naomi is shy. She **enjoys** / **dislikes** meeting new people.

5. Enrico likes to stay home. He **enjoys** / **dislikes** going out.

4 Write the opposites.

| dislike | outgoing | quiet | stay home |

1. shy: _____*outgoing*_____   3. go out: _____

2. noisy: _____   4. like: _____

5 Listen. Then check four things that Ruben enjoys doing.

TRACK 4

☐ going to parties   ☐ fixing old cars

☐ reading books   ☐ listening to music

☐ learning new dances   ☐ talking about movies

LESSON B Verbs + gerunds

Study the chart and explanation on page 126.

1 Read the chart. Complete the sentences. Use gerunds.

	Francisco	**Erika**	**Chang**
playing soccer	✓✓	✓	✓
doing homework	✓	X	O
getting up early	O	O	XX

Key	✓ = like	✓✓ = love	X = dislike	XX = hate	O = not mind

1. Chang hates _____*getting up early*_____.

2. Erika dislikes _____.

3. Chang doesn't mind _____.

4. Francisco loves _____.

5. Erika and Chang like _____.

6. Francisco and Erika don't mind _____.

2 Circle the correct answers. Use the information in Exercise 1.

1. Does Francisco like doing homework? (Yes, he does.) / No, he doesn't.

2. Does Erika dislike getting up early? Yes, she does. / No, she doesn't.

3. Does Chang dislike doing homework? Yes, he does. / No, he doesn't.

4. Do Erika and Chang like playing soccer? Yes, they do. / No, they don't.

5. Does Chang like getting up early? Yes, he does. / No, he doesn't.

6. Does Francisco mind getting up early? Yes, he does. / No, he doesn't.

Check your answers. See page 134.

3 **Complete the sentences. Use gerunds.**

| be | do | go out | listen | play | read | surf | work |

Antonio loves <u>*going out*</u> with his friends. He hates _____
1   2
alone. In English class, he likes _____ in small groups. He doesn't
3
mind _____ a textbook or _____ to a CD. He dislikes
4   5
_____ homework. On the weekend, Antonio and his friends enjoy
6
_____ soccer. They also like _____ the Internet.
7   8

4 **Complete the questions. Then write answers. Use the information in Exercise 3.**

1. **A** Does Antonio like <u>*going out*</u> with his friends?
(go out)
   B <u>*Yes, he does*</u> .

2. **A** Does he hate _____ alone?
(be)
   B _____ .

3. **A** Does he mind _____ a textbook?
(read)
   B _____ .

4. **A** Does he like _____ homework?
(do)
   B _____ .

5 **Write *Yes* / *No* questions. Use gerunds.**

1. you / enjoy / go to the beach
   <u>*Do you enjoy going to the beach*</u> ?

2. you / dislike / stand in line
   _____ ?

3. you / like / play cards
   _____ ?

4. you / mind / take out the garbage
   _____ ?

LESSON C Comparisons

Study the explanation on page 132.

1 Read the paragraph. Then complete the chart.

> Angela likes <u>socializing</u> with her friends as much as <u>playing</u> sports.
> She likes <u>dancing</u> more than cooking. She likes <u>watching</u> movies less
> than <u>cooking</u>, but she likes <u>reading</u> less than <u>watching</u> movies.

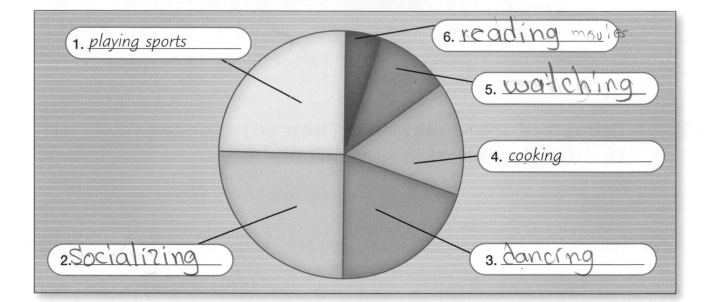

1. _playing sports_
2. Socializing
3. dancing
4. _cooking_
5. watching
6. reading movies

2 Write sentences about Angelina.

1. cooking / watching movies (less than)

   Angelina likes watching movies less than cooking.

2. watching movies / reading (more than)

   Angelina likes watching more than reading.

3. dancing / cooking (less than)

   Angelina likes cooking less than dancing.

4. dancing / socializing with friends (more than)

   Angelina socializing with friends more than dancing

5. playing sports / socializing with friends (as much as)

   Angelina likes socializing with friends as much as playing sports.

Check your answers. See page 134.

3 **Complete the sentences about the people in the pictures. Use *more than*.**

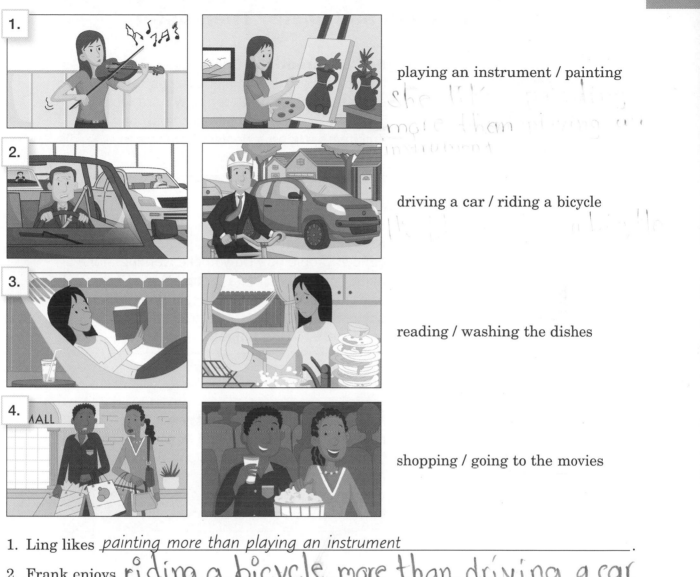

playing an instrument / painting

she lik...
more than ...
instrument

driving a car / riding a bicycle

reading / washing the dishes

shopping / going to the movies

1. Ling likes *painting more than playing an instrument* .
2. Frank enjoys riding a bicycle more than driving a car.
3. Suzanna enjoys reading more than washing the dishes.
4. Annie and Steve like going to the movies more than shopping.

4 **Look at the pictures in Exercise 3. Add the missing word in each sentence.**

1. Annie and Steve like shopping less *than* watching movies. (than)

2. Ling likes playing an instrument *less* than painting. (less)

3. Suzanna enjoys washing the dishes less *than* reading. (than)

4. Frank enjoys riding a bicycle *more* than driving a car. (more)

Check your answers. See page 134.

LESSON D Reading

1 Look at the pictures. Predict the job that each ad will describe. Read and write. Then listen.

1.

Are you creative? Do you like imagining things? Do you love making things? Do you enjoy thinking of new ideas? We are looking for creative people to join our team of architects. Help us design exciting new homes. Your future is with us!

Job: ___architect___

2.

Are you intellectual? Do you enjoy solving difficult problems? Do you like working alone more than working in a group? Yes? Then you are the right person for us! We need computer programmers to help create new computers for the future.

Job: _____

3.

Are you friendly and outgoing? Do you like talking with people and helping others? Do you enjoy meeting people and finding out about them? If your answer is yes, then teaching is the job for you. Come and join our friendly team of teachers. Apply today!

Job: _____

2 Read the ads in Exercise 1. Write the best job for each person.

1. Phil is creative. _____architect_____

2. Beverley is intellectual. _____

3. Sarah is outgoing. _____

4. Michael likes working alone. _____

5. Elena enjoys meeting new people. _____

6. Julio loves imagining new ideas. _____

Check your answers. See page 134.

3 **Match the jobs with the activities. Use the information from the ads in Exercise 1.**

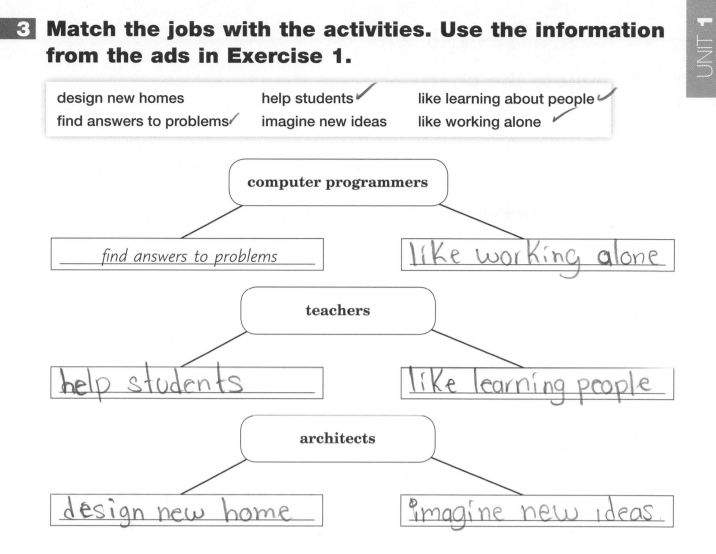

design new homes   help students ✓   like learning about people ✓
find answers to problems ✓   imagine new ideas   like working alone ✓

computer programmers

find answers to problems   like working alone

teachers

help students   like learning people

architects

design new home   imagine new ideas.

4 **Complete the sentences.**

artist   creative   friendly   intellectual   outgoing   personality   type

1. Your _____ is the way you think, feel, and act.

2. Su-lin likes thinking and finding answers. She is _____.

3. Osman enjoys making things. He is _____.

4. Jenny loves painting and drawing. She wants to be an _____.

5. Ann enjoys meeting people and doing things. She is _____.

6. Jim's personality _____ is intellectual.

7. Albert likes talking to people and socializing. He's very friendly _____.

LESSON E Writing

1 Complete the chart.

architect	drawing	helpful	reliable	surfing the Internet
creative	finding answers	helping people	scientist	talking
designer	friendly	outgoing	social worker	teacher

Jobs	Personality adjectives	Activities
architect		

2 Read the paragraph. Then complete the award.

My friend Peter Jones is a social worker at the community center in our town. He is the winner of our town's "Employee of the Month" award. Peter is very friendly and outgoing. He enjoys meeting and helping people who come to the community center. He is also very hardworking. I think Peter has the right job for his personality type.

TOWN EMPLOYEE OF THE MONTH AWARD

Name: Peter Jones

Job: _____

Place of work: _____

Personality: _____

Likes: _____

Check your answers. See page 134.

3 **Read the chart. Then complete the sentences.**

Name:	Rosa Jamulka
Job:	computer programmer
Place of work:	home
Personality:	reliable and intellectual, careful and hardworking
Likes:	surfing the Internet, finding answers to problems

Rosa Jamulka has the right job for her personality. She's a

computer programmer. She works at home. Rosa is a very reliable and

<u>intellectual</u> person. She is also careful and <u>hardworking</u>.
1   3

She loves surfing the Internet, and she enjoys <u>finding answer</u> to
                                                                4

problems. Computer programming is a good job for her since it fits her personality.

4 **Read the profile. Write a paragraph about Romano's job and personality type.**

Romano Pereira's Blog Profile

Age: 33
Gender: male
Job: architect at New Designs Company
Place of work: Raleigh, North Carolina

About me
• creative and helpful
• enjoy drawing
• like imagining things that are new and different

My Photo

Romano Pereira's job fits his personality.

_____

_____

_____

Check your answers. See page 134.

LESSON F Another view

1 **Read the questions. Look at the ads. Then fill in the correct answers.**

1.
Friendly but shy SF (age 37, 5'6") loves working in the garden, cooking, and reading. Seeking honest, good-looking SM or DM for quiet evenings at home.

2.
Intelligent DM (age 60, 5'10") loves watching movies, listening to music, and eating good food. Seeking fun-loving SF with a good heart to share a home together.

3.
Active, outgoing DM (age 28, 6'2") enjoys traveling, jogging, and camping outdoors. Seeking warm and intelligent SF under 30 for romantic trips together.

4.
Caring, kind DF (age 29, 5'5") loves driving, swimming, and spending time outdoors. Seeking friendly SM for bike trips and walks on the beach.

SM = single male, **SF** = single female, **DM** = divorced male, **DF** = divorced female

1. The older man enjoys ____.
   Ⓐ traveling
   Ⓑ camping
   ● watching movies
   Ⓓ going to the beach

2. The younger woman enjoys ____.
   Ⓐ swimming
   Ⓑ gardening
   Ⓒ cooking
   Ⓓ staying home

3. What word does NOT describe the younger man?
   Ⓐ shy
   Ⓑ active
   Ⓒ outgoing
   Ⓓ divorced

4. Which two people like going out more than staying home?
   Ⓐ 1 and 2
   Ⓑ 2 and 3
   Ⓒ 1 and 4
   Ⓓ 3 and 4

5. What does the single female enjoy doing?
   Ⓐ traveling
   Ⓑ swimming
   Ⓒ cooking
   Ⓓ driving

6. How tall is the single female?
   Ⓐ 5 feet 5 inches
   Ⓑ 5 feet 6 inches
   Ⓒ 5 feet 10 inches
   Ⓓ 6 feet 2 inches

Check your answers. See page 135.

2 Read the situation. Circle the letter of the best answer. Write a sentence with *must*.

1. Ruben doesn't like parties. He enjoys quiet evenings at home.
   a. be fun-loving
   b. be very friendly
   c. be a little shy
   d. be very outgoing

   Ruben must be a little shy .

2. Miguel plays guitar in a band. He's also a pretty good singer.
   a. love music
   b. know how to dance
   c. be an honest person
   d. like to be alone

   _____ .

3. Adriana loves math. She's studying computer science. She gets good grades.
   a. be a kind person
   b. be a little shy
   c. be good at sports
   d. be very intelligent

   _____ .

4. In the summer, Hana takes tennis lessons. In the winter, she likes to go skiing.
   a. like sports a lot
   b. like spending weekends at home
   c. be a quiet, shy person
   d. be a good dancer

   _____ .

3 Complete the sentences. Use words from the box and *must* or *must not*.

be a reliable employee	be very creative	like working out
be a very good cook	know how to swim	

1. No one likes Julia's food. Her cakes are terrible, and she can't even make good sandwiches. She *must not be a very good cook* _____ .

2. Vincent likes art and music a lot. That's one of his paintings on the wall.
   He _____ .

3. Malcom is often late for work. At work, he spends time talking on his cell phone and surfing the Internet. He _____ .

4. Melinda never exercises. She doesn't like going for walks in the park.
   She _____ .

5. In the summer, Abby goes to the beach or to the pool almost every day.
   She _____ .

Check your answers. See page 135. **UNIT 1** 17

LESSON A Listening

1 Complete the conversation. Then listen.

TRACK 6

| concentrate | discouraged | index cards | list | paper | underline |

VICTOR Hi, Frank. How's it going?

FRANK Not so good. Can you help me? I have so much homework. I have to write a
_____paper_____ for Monday, and I have a test tomorrow!
   1

VICTOR You need to make a _____list_____ of all your homework. Then write the due
   2
date of each item on your calendar.

FRANK OK, but what about the test?

VICTOR You should study your textbook and concetrate all the main ideas. Write the
   3
important words on index cards and study them in your free time. Do you
   4
live near a quiet place where you can underline ?
   5

FRANK Well, there's a library a few blocks away.

VICTOR Good! You should study and write your paper there. Don't feel discouraged!
   6

---

2 Circle the correct answers. Use the information in Exercise 1.

1. Frank needs some _b_.
   a. homework
   b. advice
   c. friends
   d. paper

2. Frank has to _c_.
   a. study less
   b. help Victor
   c. plan his work
   d. get a calendar

3. Victor is _c_.
   a. boring
   b. helpful
   c. discouraged
   d. quiet

4. Victor tells Frank how to _b_.
   a. do his homework
   b. concentrate
   c. get to the library
   d. write a paper

Check your answers. See page 135.

3 Match the sentences.

1. Tami can't finish her book. __d__
2. Bernie underlines the main ideas. __a__
3. Sue can't remember new words. __f__
4. Pam has too much homework. __e__
5. Paolo is not happy. __d__
6. The book isn't interesting. __C__

a. He is an active reader.
b. He is discouraged.
c. It's boring.
d. She needs to concentrate.
e. She needs to make a list of things to do.
f. She needs to write them on index cards.

4 Complete the sentences.

active	concentrate	index cards	paper
boring	discouraged	list	underline

1. I have to make a _____list_____ of all my homework.
2. I have to finish this ____paper____ by tomorrow morning.
3. It's hard to __index cards__ in this noisy room.
4. I really need to be a more ____active____ reader.
5. I need to ____concentrate____ all the main ideas in this article.
6. I will write the most important information on ____underline____.
7. This book is ____boring____. I can't read it.
8. I feel __discouraged__ because I never know all of the answers.

5 Mark an ✗ next to the bad study habits. Put a (✓) next to the good study habits.

[✗] doesn't study new words
[✗] is late for class
[✗] hands in homework late
[✓] makes to-do lists

[✓] forgets homework
[✗] doesn't study for tests
[✗] writes new words on index cards
[✓] underlines the main ideas

6 Listen. Then check (✓) the statement that is true.

TRACK 7

☐ Amelia thinks Mr. Wilson's strategies are crazy.
☐ Mr. Wilson thinks that Amelia is not a very good student.
☐ Mr. Wilson has talked about learning strategies in class.

LESSON B Present perfect

Study the chart and explanation on page 128. For a list of irregular verbs, turn to page 131.

1 Circle *for* or *since*.

1. I have known Elsa (for)/ **since** two years.

2. Tina has taught this class **for /** (**since**) September.

3. Jasmine has worked in the store **for /** (**since**) last year.

4. We have lived in Miami (**for**) / **since** six months.

5. Kelly has had her car **for / since** 2010.

6. They have been in the library **for / since** 4:00 p.m.

7. I have studied computers **for / since** two weeks.

8. They have been in our class **for / since** Tuesday.

2 Complete the sentences. Use *have* or *has*.

1. How long _____*have*_____ you had your car?

2. How long _____ I known you?

3. How long _____ she studied Spanish?

4. How long _____ they lived in this city?

5. How long _____ he been in Canada?

6. How long _____ we worked here?

3 Complete the sentences. Use the present perfect.

1. Bianca works in a restaurant. She _____*has worked*_____ there for five years.

2. Federico and Sonya live in Brazil. They _____ there since April.

3. My sister and I study piano. We _____ piano for 15 years.

4. Mei-lin has a motorcycle. She _____ a motorcycle since 2011.

5. Ms. Green teaches English. She _____ English for twelve years.

6. Tom is a student. He _____ a student for three months.

Check your answers. See page 135.

4 Complete the sentences. Write the answers.

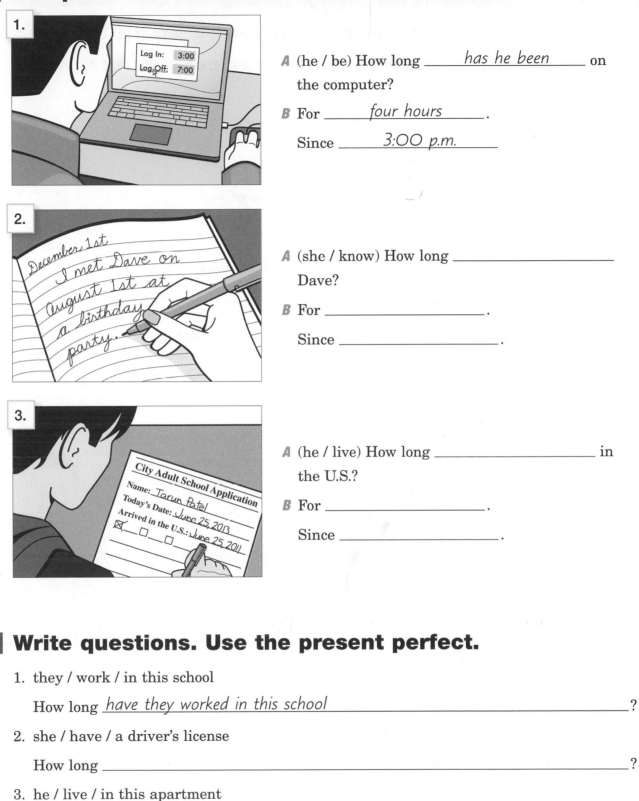

1.

Log In: 3:00
Log Off: 7:00

A (he / be) How long _____*has he been*_____ on the computer?

B For _____*four hours*_____ .

Since _____*3:00 p.m.*_____

2.

December 1st
I met Dave on
August 1st at
a birthday
party.

A (she / know) How long _____ Dave?

B For _____ .

Since _____ .

3.

City Adult School Application
Name: *Tarun Patel*
Today's Date: *June 25, 2013*
☒ ☐ ☐ Arrived in the U.S.: *June 25, 2011*

A (he / live) How long _____ in the U.S.?

B For _____ .

Since _____ .

5 Write questions. Use the present perfect.

1. they / work / in this school

   How long _*have they worked in this school*_____?

2. she / have / a driver's license

   How long _____?

3. he / live / in this apartment

   How long _____?

4. you / be / married

   How long _____?

LESSON C Present perfect

Study the chart and explanation on page 128. For a list of irregular verbs, turn to page 131.

1 Complete the sentences. Use the correct form of the verb.

1. Have you ever _____ *lost* _____ a library book?
   (lose)
2. Has your teacher ever _____ forgotten _____ your name?
   (forget)
3. Have you ever _____ read _____ the newspaper online?
   (read)
4. Have you ever _____ taken _____ the bus to school?
   (take)
5. Have you ever _____ gotten _____ the best grade in the class?
   (get)

2 Read the chart. Complete the sentences.

	Study skills survey: Do you . . .	Janice	Hiroshi
1.	study English online?	yes	no
2.	talk to a school counselor?	no	no
3.	make to-do lists?	yes	no
4.	write new words in a vocabulary notebook?	yes	yes
5.	do your homework on the computer?	yes	no

1. A ___ Has ___ Janice ever ___ studied ___ English online?

   B ___ Yes, she has ___ .

2. A ___ Have ___ Janice and Hiroshi ever ___ talken ___ to a school counselor?

   B Yes, they haven't

3. A Has ___ Janice ever ___ made ___ a to-do list?

   B Yes, she has .

4. A Have ___ Janice and Hiroshi ever written ___ new words in a vocabulary notebook?

   B Yes, they have .

5. A Has ___ Hiroshi ever ___ done ___ his homework on the computer?

   B No, He hasn't

Check your answers. See page 135.

3 Complete the sentences. Use *ever*.

1. ___*Have you ever used*___ the computer in the library?
   (you, use)

2. <u>Has your teacher ever talken</u> to you after class?
   (your teacher, talk)

3. <u>Have your friend ever studied</u> with you?
   (your friends, study)

4. <u>Have you ever written</u> an e-mail to your teacher?
   (you, write)

5. <u>Have you ever underline</u> the main ideas in your textbook?
   (you, underline)

6. <u>Have you ever gotten</u> all the questions correct on a test?
   (you, get)

4 Read the conversations. Write sentences about the people in the conversations.

1. **KATE** Have you ever forgotten to study for a test?

   MELISSA No, I haven't.

   KATE Have you ever lost your textbook?

   MELISSA Yes, I have. I left it on a bus.

   Melissa hasn't ever forgotten to study for a test.

   She has lost her textbook.

2. **LUIS** Have you ever had trouble concentrating on your homework?

   FRANCO Yes!

   LUIS Have you ever done the wrong homework?

   FRANCO No, I don't think so.

   <u>Franco has ever had trouble concentrating on your homework</u>
   <u>He hasn't done the wrong homework.</u>

3. **MARIA** Have you ever read a newspaper in English?

   ROSE Yes, I have.

   MARIA Have you ever tried to speak English with your neighbors?

   ROSE No, I haven't. But I want to!

   <u>Rose has ever read a newspaper in English</u>
   <u>She hasn't ever tried to speak English with your neighbors.</u>

Check your answers. See page 135. **UNIT 2 23**

LESSON D Reading

1 **Read and answer the questions. Then listen.**

Strategies for Learning New Words

Have you ever felt discouraged because there are so many new words to learn in English? Have you tried to set goals for learning new words? Here are some ideas to help you practice and remember vocabulary.

Strategy #1: Keep a vocabulary notebook.
Buy a small notebook. Take it with you everywhere. When you see new words around you in the street, in an advertisement, or in a newspaper, write the new words in your notebook. Use clues to guess the meanings. At the end of the day, use your dictionary to check the meanings. Write an example sentence, or draw a picture to help you remember the new words.

Strategy #2: Make vocabulary cards.
Have you ever felt bored waiting in line or taking the bus? Use the time to practice vocabulary. Choose five words from your English class or from a newspaper or magazine. Write each word on a small card. Write the word on one side of the card. Then write the definition or a translation on the other side. Test yourself on the definitions.

Strategy #3: Use new words in conversations every day.
Choose one new word from your notebook or vocabulary cards every day. Try to use it in a conversation some time during the day with your friends, classmates, family, or with your teacher. Using the words you learn will help you remember them.

1. What is the article about?

   The article is about strategies for learning new words.

2. What are the three strategies described in this article?

   1. _____

   2. _____

   3. _____

3. If you write a new word on one side of a card and write the definition on the other side, what strategy are you using?

   _____

Check your answers. See page 135.

2 Circle the correct answers. Use the information in Exercise 1.

1. The article says you can use *all* of these strategies ____ .
   a. in class
   b. every day *(circled)*
   c. on the bus
   d. with pictures

2. The article says these strategies should help you to ____ new words.
   a. draw
   b. write
   c. translate
   d. remember

3. The article says you should use ____ to check definitions.
   a. a dictionary
   b. a notebook
   c. an index card
   d. an advertisement

4. The article says you can practice using new words when ____ .
   a. watching TV
   b. talking to friends
   c. listening to the radio
   d. reading a newspaper

3 Make sentences. Match the sentence parts. Use the information in Exercise 1.

1. You can draw pictures *c*
2. You can use new words ____
3. You can look at vocabulary cards ____
4. You should guess the meaning first ____
5. You should write definitions ____

a. and use a dictionary later.
b. on the back of vocabulary cards.
c. in your vocabulary notebook.
d. when you talk to friends.
e. when you are waiting in line.

4 Look at the bold words. Write a word from the box with a similar meaning.

clues	gestures	plan	practice	set	strategies

1. The article suggests some easy **methods** for learning new words. *strategies*

2. I need to **decide on** a few goals for learning English. _____

3. Have you made a **decision** to help you reach your goals? _____

4. I need to **use** new words every day to help me remember them. _____

5. Certain **information** in a sentence can help you guess the meaning. _____

6. **Hand movements** can sometimes help to explain the meaning. _____

LESSON E Writing

1 Complete the charts.

Ask questions in class every day.	Underline new words with colored pens.
Listen to the radio.	Use new words in everyday conversation.
Look up new words in a dictionary.	Watch movies in English.
Read newspapers in English.	Watch the news in English.
Talk to people at work in English.	

Listening strategies	Speaking strategies	Reading strategies
Listen to the radio.		

2 Read Omar's journal. Then answer the questions.

I want to improve my reading in English. One strategy is to read newspapers or magazines in English. For example, I'm going to read a newspaper article in English every day. I'm also going to use colored pens to underline new words. For example, I'll use a yellow pen for new and difficult words and a blue pen when I can guess the meaning. Another strategy is to use my dictionary more often. I will choose five words I don't know each day and check the meanings in my dictionary. If I practice these strategies, I will improve my English reading skills.

1. What is Omar's first strategy for improving his reading? Give an example.

   Omar's first strategy is to read newspapers or magazines in English.

   He is going to read a newspaper article in English every day.

2. What is Omar's second strategy for improving his reading? Give an example.

   _____

   _____

3. What is Omar's third strategy for improving his reading? Give an example.

   _____

   _____

Check your answers. See page 135.

3 **Read the strategies. Write the number of the strategy next to the example.**

Strategy 1: Guess the meaning of new words.
Strategy 2: Use one new word every day.
Strategy 3: Make a vocabulary notebook.
Strategy 4: Review new words after class.

__4__ 1. I'll make vocabulary cards and look at them on the bus.

_____ 2. I'll write the new word in a sentence and send it in an e-mail to my friend.

_____ 3. I'll write three new words in my notebook every day.

_____ 4. I can look at the pictures and sentences around a new word and figure out the meaning.

4 **Write a paragraph about four strategies for learning new words. Give one example for each strategy. Use the strategies and examples in Exercise 3.**

I have learned some useful strategies for learning new words.

_____

_____

_____

_____

_____

_____

_____

_____

_____

_____

_____

_____

_____

LESSON F Another view

1 Complete the sentences.

answer   look   make   read   skim   spend   worry

Test-taking tips

1. _____Read_____ the directions carefully.

2. _____ the whole test before you start.

3. _____ the most difficult questions at the end.

4. Don't _____ too much time on one question.

5. Don't _____ if the other students finish before you.

6. _____ sure you have answered all questions on the test.

7. Don't _____ at other students' tests.

2 Which tips did these students need to follow? Write the number of the tip from Exercise 1.

1. I spent 20 minutes on the first question, and I didn't have time to finish the other questions. Tip _4_

2. Everyone finished before me, and I started to worry. Tip _____

3. I forgot to answer some of the questions. Tip _____

4. I tried to look at another student's test, and I failed the test. Tip _____

5. I didn't know the test had three parts. I only finished two parts. Tip _____

6. I spent too much time on the difficult questions. I wasn't able to answer the easy questions. Tip _____

7. I circled the answers, but the directions said: "Underline the answers." Tip _____

Check your answers. See page 135.

3 Complete the story. Use the correct words.

Vicky _____*has been*_____ a student at the City
       (1. was / has been)
University for two years. She _____
             (2. always got / has always gotten)
good grades, but since last January, her grades

_____ down. Why? Well, in
(3. went / have gone)
January, she _____ a problem. She
         (4. had / has had)
_____ more money to pay for school and
(5. needed / has needed)
for rent. So, on January 10th, she _____ a job as a server at a
          (6. started / has started)
café near the school. She _____ there for two months now. Last
       (7. worked / has worked)
week, Vicky _____ to her school counselor about the problem and
     (8. talked / has talked)
asked, "How can I work and study at the same time?" In their meeting, the counselor

_____ her some good ideas about organizing her time. Since then,
(9. gave / has given)
her grades _____, and she's still working.
(10. improved / have improved)

4 Complete the sentences. Use the present perfect or the simple past. Use the information in the chart.

	Naomi	Tran
1. forget to put (his / her) name on a test		on a history test last week
2. watch a TV show in English	the news on TV last night	
3. study geometry	in the first year of high school	in the first year of high school

1. Has Tran ever forgotten to put his name on a test?

    Yes. He _____ .

2. _____ Naomi ever _____ ?

    Yes. _____ .

3. _____ Naomi and Tran ever _____ ?

    Yes. _____ .

LESSON A Listening

1 Read and complete the paragraph. Then listen.

TRACK 9

| borrow | broken | came over | complain | favor | noisy |

I Owe You One

My neighbor Amy _____*came over*_____ yesterday to ask a _____.
                        1   2

Her light was _____, and it was too high for her to reach. She wanted
                        3

to _____ my ladder. We had a cup of coffee and started to talk about
           4

our other neighbors. Two weeks ago, they had a party, and Amy told them the music

was too loud. Then, last weekend, they had another party. Amy couldn't sleep because

they were too _____. I said she should _____ to the
                        5   6

building manager, and I gave her the phone number. Then I helped her carry my ladder

to her apartment. "Rita, thanks for your help," she said. "I owe you one!"

2 Circle the correct answers. Use the information in Exercise 1.

1. Amy asked Rita for a ____.
   a. ladder
   b. new light
   c. phone number
   d. cup of coffee

2. Amy couldn't sleep because ____.
   a. her light was broken
   b. the neighbors had a party
   c. she needed to call the manager
   d. she needed to borrow a ladder

3. Amy ____ Rita's help.
   a. doesn't need
   b. doesn't want
   c. complains about
   d. really appreciates

4. Amy owes Rita a ____.
   a. favor
   b. ladder
   c. phone number
   d. cup of coffee

Check your answers. See page 135.

3 Complete the sentences.

appreciates	come over	favor	noisy
borrow	complained	noise	owe

1. Mary hasn't read this book. She is going to ___borrow___ it from me.

2. The neighbors are not quiet. They are _____ all the time.

3. Meg thanked Tina for her help. She always _____ Tina's help.

4. You lent me 10 dollars. Here's a dollar. I now _____ you nine dollars.

5. My neighbors were so noisy last night. I _____ to the apartment manager.

6. Our old dishwasher made a lot of _____. Our new one is quiet.

7. Could you do me a _____ and babysit my children tonight?

8. My daughter wants her friend to _____, but I said no. It's a school night.

4 Circle the correct word.

Prestado
1. Rita (lent)/ borrowed a ladder to Amy.
   prestado/da
2. Amy lent / **borrowed** a ladder from Rita.

3. My friend lent / **borrowed** a book from me.

4. I **lent** / borrowed a book to my friend.

5 Complete the sentences. Use *lend* or *borrow*.

1. Could you ___lend___ me some money? I want to buy a cup of coffee.

2. I can't __lent__ you my cell phone right now. It's broken.

3. Could I __borrowed__ your dictionary? I forgot how to spell this word.

4. Do you want to __borrowed__ my umbrella? It's raining outside.

6 How is Daniel going to get into his apartment? Listen and check.

TRACK 10

☐ His wife is going to come home and open the door.

☐ His neighbor, Edgar, has a copy of his key.

☐ He's going to borrow a key from the building manager.

LESSON B Phrases and clauses with *because*

Study the explanation on page 132.

1 Make sentences. Match the sentence parts.

1. Stan borrowed some money __c__
2. Dan travels a lot __d__
3. Alfredo and Maria were late __e__
4. Dolores studied for three hours __b__
5. Tran called the building manager __a__

a. because of his job.
b. because she had a big test.
c. because he wants to buy a car.
d. because his window was broken.
e. because of a flat tire.

2 Circle *because* or *because of*.

1. Ana couldn't sleep (because) / because of the baby was crying.

2. I couldn't go to work **because** / because of my car broke down.

3. We didn't go out because / **because of** the bad weather.

4. Tanya needed a ladder because / **because of** the broken light.

5. Joseph couldn't take a vacation because / **because of** his busy work schedule.

6. Marietta didn't come to class **because** / because of she had a bad headache.

3 Rewrite the sentences. Use the words in parentheses.

1. We couldn't sleep *because it was noisy*. (the noise)

   We couldn't sleep because of the noise.

2. We couldn't play soccer *because it was raining*. (the rain)

   We couldn't play soccer because of the rain.

3. They were late for the appointment *because there were a lot of cars*. (the traffic)

   They were late for the appointment because of the traffic.

4. Reyna stayed at home *because she had the flu*. (the flu)

   Reyna stayed at home because of the flu.

5. Sam stayed up late *because he watched the basketball game*. (the basketball game)

   Sam stayed up late because the basketball game.

6. Beatriz moved to this country *because her children live here*. (her children)

   Beatriz moved to this country because of her children.

Check your answers. See page 136.

4 Complete the sentences. Use *because* or *because of*.

1. Teresa couldn't sleep last night _____*because*_____ she had a headache.

2. Keizo couldn't lock his door _____ he lost his keys.

3. We moved to California _____ my husband's job.

4. William couldn't drive his car _____ the broken door.

5. Karen likes her neighborhood _____ it is safe at night.

5 Complete the sentences. Use *because* or *because of* and words from the box.

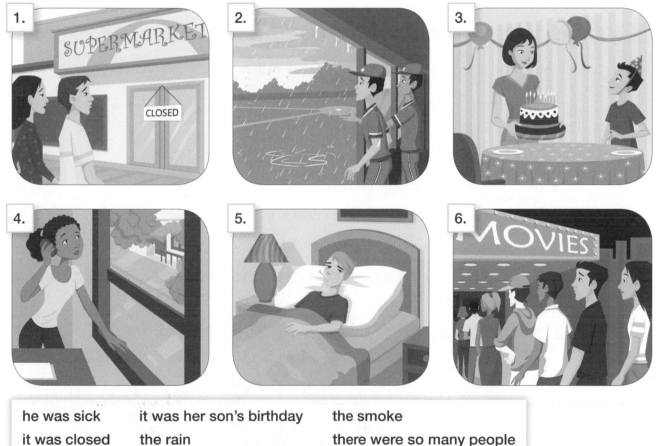

| he was sick | it was her son's birthday | the smoke |
| it was closed | the rain | there were so many people |

1. They couldn't go to the supermarket *because it was closed* _____.

2. They couldn't play baseball _____.

3. She made a cake _____.

4. My neighbor called 911 _____.

5. He couldn't go to school _____.

6. We had to wait a long time _____.

LESSON C Adverbs of degree

Study the explanation on page 132.

1 Write the opposites.

close	hot	small	strong	tall	young

1. cold   _____hot_____
2. short   _____
3. big   _____

4. weak   _____
5. far   _____
6. old   _____

2 Complete the sentences. Use the adjectives in Exercise 1.

1. The water is _____hot_____ enough to make coffee.

2. He isn't _____ enough to reach the ceiling.

3. They're not _____ enough to lift the box.

4. The car is too _____ for five people.

5. He is too _____ to get married.

6. The train station isn't _____ enough to walk.

3 Complete the sentences. Use the correct adjective and *too* or *enough*.

1. She's ___too young___ .
2. She's not _old enough_ .

3. He's _____ .
4. He's not _____ .

5. It's _____ .
6. It's not _____ .

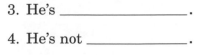

Check your answers. See page 136.

4 Complete the sentences. Use *too* or *not . . . enough* with the word in parentheses.

1. **A** I don't want to live in the city anymore. It's _____ too noisy _____.
   (noisy)

   B I agree. It's _____ not quiet enough _____.
   (quiet)

2. **A** The rent for this apartment is _____.
   (expensive)

   B You're right. It's _____.
   (cheap)

3. **A** We need a new house. Our house is _____.
   (small)

   B That's true. Our house is _____.
   (big)

4. **A** I don't like this exercise. It's _____.
   (difficult)

   B I agree. It's _____.
   (easy)

5. **A** I want to quit my job. It's _____.
   (boring)

   B You've complained to me before that your job is _____.
   (interesting)

6. **A** My daughter wants to take a trip by herself. She's _____.
   (young)

   B I agree. She's _____.
   (old)

5 Complete the sentences. Use the correct adjective and *too* or *enough*.

big	expensive	experienced	high	old	strong	tall	weak	young

1. I have five children. This house isn't _____ big enough _____ for us.

2. James is 6'10". He's _____ to reach the ceiling.

3. My daughter is six months old. She's not _____ to talk.

4. The books are on the top shelf. They're _____ to reach.

5. This box is not very heavy. I'm _____ to carry it.

6. Meredith is 14 years old. She's _____ to drive.

7. My husband hasn't finished his training. He's not _____ to be an engineer.

8. We need to buy a used car. A new car is _____ for us.

9. I need some help! I'm _____ to lift this TV.

1 Read and correct the information in the sentences. Then listen.

TRACK 11

MY NEIGHBORHOOD

People sometimes ask me about my neighborhood. Is it nice? Is it safe? My answer is that I'm very lucky to have nice neighbors. They are very friendly and kind. For example, they help me with shopping when I feel too sick to go out. They look after my house when I am away. Once a month, we get together to talk about any problems.

Last week, my neighbors saw some teenagers near my house. They were painting graffiti on a wall. My neighbors shouted at them, and they ran away. The next day, my neighbors came over with some brushes and some paint. We painted over the graffiti together, and the teens haven't come back. I am so happy that I have such nice neighbors. Because we work together, this neighborhood is a safe place to live.

1. The writer doesn't like to spend time with her neighbors.

   The writer gets together with her neighbors once a month.

2. The writer's neighbors painted graffiti.

   _____

3. The writer's neighbors talked to the teenagers, and they walked away.

   _____

4. The writer's neighborhood is not safe.

   _____

Check your answers. See page 136.

2 Circle the correct answers. Use the information in Exercise 1.

1. What is the main idea of the first paragraph?
   a. The writer's neighbors watch her house.
   b. The writer's neighbors talk every month.
   c. The writer's neighbors are friendly.
   d. The writer's neighbors are too noisy.

2. The writer gives examples to show that ____.
   a. her neighbors are nice people
   b. her neighbors talk too much
   c. she has very few neighbors
   d. she has a lot of neighbors

3. What did the neighbors see?
   a. teenagers talking
   b. teenagers painting graffiti
   c. teenagers breaking a window
   d. teenagers breaking into the writer's house

4. What did the neighbors do?
   a. They ran away.
   b. They called the police.
   c. They stayed in their houses.
   d. They shouted at the teenagers.

3 Complete the sentences.

break into	get into	get together	goes off	look after	run away

1. You can _____ get into _____ my car and wait for me. Here's the key.

2. When do you want to _____ again?

3. My neighbors _____ my dog when I'm on vacation.

4. My smoke alarm sometimes _____ when I am cooking.

5. I close the windows so my cat can't _____ .

6. Someone tried to _____ my car yesterday, so I called the police.

4 Look at the bold words. Write verbs from Exercise 3 with a similar meaning.

1. The men tried to **escape** when they saw the police car. _____ run away _____

2. I **take care of** my neighbor's children in the afternoon. _____

3. My friends and I often **meet** at a coffee shop after class. _____

4. My alarm clock **makes a loud noise** at 6:00 every morning. _____

5. My shoes are very dirty. I shouldn't **enter** your car. _____

6. Someone tried to **enter** my home last night, so I called the police. _____

LESSON E Writing

1 Read the letter. Label the parts of the letter.

| problem | request | signature | today's date |

1. _today's date_

2. _____

3. _____

4. _____

July 15, 2013
_____

Century Building Management
1000 Chestnut Street
Miami, FL 33127

To Whom It May Concern:

My name is Nazmi Akerjee. I live at 310 Walnut Street in Apartment 5. I am writing because the hallway outside my apartment has a broken light. I tried to fix it, but my ladder is not tall enough to reach it. The hallway is not safe at night because of the broken light.

Could you please come as soon as possible to fix the light? Thank you in advance for your help.

Sincerely,

Nazmi Akerjee

Nazmi Akerjee

2 Circle *T* (True) or *F* (False). Use the information in Exercise 1.

1. Nazmi knows the name of the person to whom she is writing.   T   (F)
2. Nazmi's address is 310 Chestnut Street, Apartment 5.   T   F
3. The broken light is inside Nazmi's apartment.   T   F
4. Nazmi feels that her hallway is not safe at night.   T   F
5. Nazmi wants someone to fix the light.   T   F
6. Nazmi tried to fix the light.   T   F
7. The ladder is tall enough to reach the light.   T   F
8. Century Building Management is at 1000 Chestnut Street.   T   F

Check your answers. See page 136.

3 Complete the sentences.

advance	because	because of	soon	too

1. Could you please send a repair person as _____*soon*_____ as possible?

2. I am writing _____ my window is broken.

3. It is _____ cold for me to sleep in the apartment.

4. Thank you in _____ for fixing the problem.

5. My apartment is very cold _____ the broken window.

4 Write a letter of complaint about a broken window. Use the information in Exercise 3.

_____

Prestige Apartments
286 10th Street
Burlington, VT 05401

_____ :

My name is _____

_____

_____

_____

_____

_____

_____

_____

_____

Sincerely,

_____

Read the questions. Look at the ad. Then fill in the correct answers.

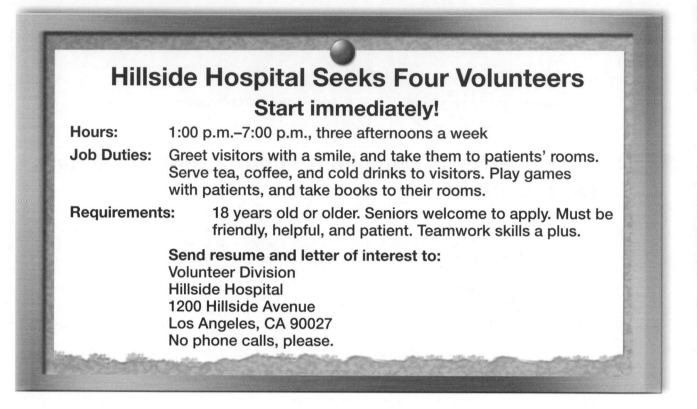

Hillside Hospital Seeks Four Volunteers
Start immediately!

Hours:	1:00 p.m.–7:00 p.m., three afternoons a week
Job Duties:	Greet visitors with a smile, and take them to patients' rooms. Serve tea, coffee, and cold drinks to visitors. Play games with patients, and take books to their rooms.
Requirements:	18 years old or older. Seniors welcome to apply. Must be friendly, helpful, and patient. Teamwork skills a plus.

Send resume and letter of interest to:
Volunteer Division
Hillside Hospital
1200 Hillside Avenue
Los Angeles, CA 90027
No phone calls, please.

1. Volunteers must be ⎯⎯ years old.
   ● at least 18
   Ⓑ over 65
   Ⓒ under 18
   Ⓓ under 65

2. How many hours do volunteers have to work a day?
   Ⓐ one
   Ⓑ three
   Ⓒ six
   Ⓓ seven

3. Which statement is NOT true?
   Ⓐ Volunteers should be patient.
   Ⓑ Volunteers should be very friendly.
   Ⓒ Volunteers should be experienced nurses.
   Ⓓ Volunteers should like meeting people.

4. What will a volunteer at the hospital do?
   Ⓐ assist nurses
   Ⓑ assist visitors
   Ⓒ give medicine
   Ⓓ serve food

5. How many days a week do volunteers have to work?
   Ⓐ one
   Ⓑ three
   Ⓒ four
   Ⓓ seven

6. Which statement is true?
   Ⓐ Volunteers must prefer to work alone.
   Ⓑ Volunteers must like meeting people.
   Ⓒ Volunteers must call to apply.
   Ⓓ Volunteers must like children.

Check your answers. See page 136.

2 **Complete the sentences. Use the affirmative or negative of *be able to*.**

1. We ___aren't able to do___ the laundry today. The washing machine is broken.
   (do)

2. Most people in Quebec _____ two languages — French and English.
   (speak)

3. They're complaining because they _____ a conversation. It's too noisy
   (have)
   in here.

4. My neighbor has a set of my keys. She _____ my door if I lose my keys.
   (open)

5. The technician _____ my computer now. I have to wait until tomorrow.
   (fix)

6. I'm sorry, but Tom _____ here today. He's too busy.
   (be)

7. They _____ the apartment now because it has a new smoke alarm.
   (rent)

8. I _____ the office at 5:00 today. I have too much work to do.
   (leave)

3 **Write sentences that are true for you. Use *be able to* and the words in parentheses.**

1. (run a mile in 10 minutes)
   ___I'm able to run a mile in 10 minutes.___ OR ___I'm not able to run a mile in 10 minutes___

2. (lift 10 pounds with one hand)
   _____

3. (speak Japanese)
   _____

4. (play the piano for my classmates)
   _____

5. (fix a computer)
   _____

6. (change a flat tire)
   _____

Check your answers. See page 136.

Health

LESSON **A** Listening

1 **Read and complete the paragraph. Then listen.**

TRACK 12

| advice | diet | exercise | gained | pressure | weight |

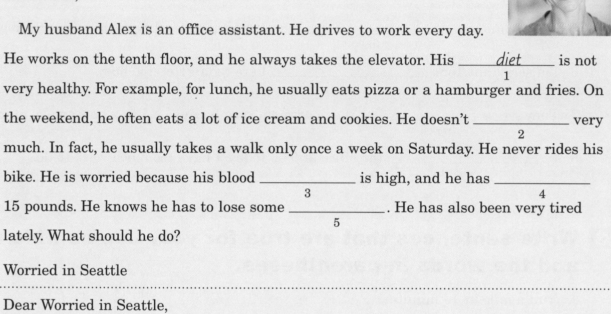

Dear Alice,

   My husband Alex is an office assistant. He drives to work every day.
He works on the tenth floor, and he always takes the elevator. His _____*diet*_____ is not
                                                                        1
very healthy. For example, for lunch, he usually eats pizza or a hamburger and fries. On
the weekend, he often eats a lot of ice cream and cookies. He doesn't _____ very
                                                                          2
much. In fact, he usually takes a walk only once a week on Saturday. He never rides his
bike. He is worried because his blood _____ is high, and he has _____
                                          3   4
15 pounds. He knows he has to lose some _____. He has also been very tired
                                             5
lately. What should he do?

Worried in Seattle

. . . .

Dear Worried in Seattle,

   Your husband needs to make an appointment to see his doctor so that he can ask the
doctor for some _____.
                      6
Alice

2 **Circle the correct answers. Use the information in Exercise 1.**

1. Alex always _____.
   a. takes the elevator
   b. walks up the stairs

2. Alex does not _____.
   a. take walks during the week
   b. exercise enough

3. Alex is worried because _____.
   a. he never rides his bike
   b. he has gained weight

4. Alice says Alex needs to _____.
   a. change his job
   b. talk to his doctor

Check your answers. See page 136.

3 Complete the chart.

check your weight	eat breakfast	go to bed late
drink a lot of soda	eat fish	ride a bicycle
eat a lot of hamburgers	gain 20 pounds	

Healthy activities	Unhealthy activities
check your weight	

4 Complete the sentences.

advice	diet	exercise	medication	weight

1. **A** Pat eats too many hamburgers. He needs to change his ____*diet*____.

   B I know.

2. **A** Alex has high blood pressure. He needs to take _____.

   B That's too bad.

3. **A** I've gained 20 pounds. I need to lose _____.

   B You should try going to the gym three times a week.

4. **A** Ali sits at work all day.

   B He needs to _____ regularly.

5. **A** I really want to stay healthy.

   B Then you need to follow your doctor's _____.

5 Listen. Then write *P* for the things Stan did in the past and *N* for the things he does now.

TRACK 13

_N_ walk up the stairs   ____ eat breakfast

____ eat fast food for lunch   ____ go to the gym

____ take the elevator   ____ work 12 hours a day

____ have soup for lunch   ____ leave work at 5:30

Check your answers. See page 136.

LESSON **B** Present perfect

Study the chart and explanation on page 128. For a list of irregular verbs, turn to page 131.

1 ## Complete the paragraph. Use the present perfect.

| be | eat | exercise | gain | give | go | start |

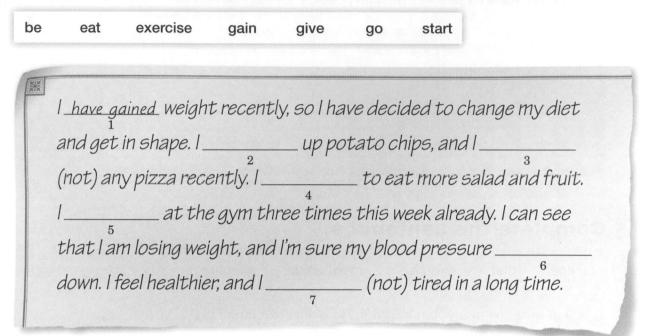

I _have gained_ weight recently, so I have decided to change my diet
1
and get in shape. I _____ up potato chips, and I _____
2   3
(not) any pizza recently. I _____ to eat more salad and fruit.
4
I _____ at the gym three times this week already. I can see
5
that I am losing weight, and I'm sure my blood pressure _____
6
down. I feel healthier, and I _____ (not) tired in a long time.
7

2 ## Write sentences. Use the present perfect.

1. You / not / exercise / this week
   You haven't exercised this week.

2. Paul / gain weight / recently
   _____

3. Ray and Louisa / lose weight / recently
   _____

4. Alicia / be unhappy / lately
   _____

5. My blood pressure / go up / recently
   _____

6. Greg / not / visit a dentist / recently
   _____

7. Sarah / give up / desserts / lately
   _____

Check your answers. See page 136.

3 Write sentences about Annette. Use the present perfect with *recently*.

> Annette's Goals for November
>
> 1. Check blood pressure.
> 2. Go to the gym. ✔
> 3. Eat more fruits and vegetables. ✔
> 4. Sleep eight hours a day. ✔
> 5. Take vitamins.

1. *Annette hasn't checked her blood pressure recently.*

2. _____

3. _____

4. _____

5. _____

4 Write questions and answers. Use the present perfect.

1. Bill / lose weight / recently

   A *Has Bill lost weight recently* _____?

   B No, _____.

2. Tina and Mario / give up desserts / recently

   A _____?

   B Yes, _____.

3. you / check your blood pressure / lately

   A _____?

   B No, _____.

4. Barbara / sleep much / lately

   A _____?

   B Yes, _____.

5. Lisa / start taking vitamins / recently

   A _____?

   B No, _____.

Check your answers. See page 136.

LESSON C *Used to*

Study the chart and explanation on page 129.

1 Circle *use* or *used*.

1. Did Angie **use** / **used** to have high blood pressure?

2. They **use** / **used** to drink a lot of coffee.

3. Tia and Arturo **use** / **used** to go to the gym every weekend.

4. Did Wesley **use** / **used** to drive to work?

5. We **use** / **used** to eat hamburgers and fries.

6. Did you **use** / **used** to feel tired all the time?

2 Complete the sentences. Use *used to* or *use to*.

1. When I was a teenager, I ____used to____ play soccer.

2. Did you _____ exercise a lot when you were young?

3. In my country, I _____ eat rice every day.

4. When I was a child, I _____ drink milk every morning.

5. Did you _____ watch TV when you were a child?

6. I _____ get up late every day, but now I get up early.

3 Complete the paragraph. Use *used to* or the simple present tense.

Samantha _____used to eat_____ a lot of chocolate and ice cream.
                          1. eat
Now, she _____eats_____ a lot of fruit and _____
              2. eat   3. take
vitamins every day. She _____ only once a week, but now she
                                    4. exercise
_____ to the gym three times a week. She _____
          5. go   6. drive
to work, but now she _____ a bike. She _____
                              7. ride   8. drink
a lot of coffee, but now she _____ tea or fruit juice. She
                                    9. drink
_____ tired all the time, but now she _____
          10. feel   11. have
a lot of energy. Samantha has changed her habits and feels much better now.

Check your answers. See page 136.

4 Read the chart. Write sentences about Emilia.

	Before	Now
1.	Stay up until 2:00 a.m.	Go to bed at 10:00 p.m.
2.	Eat meat every day	Eat fish twice a week
3.	Go straight home after work	Go to the gym three times a week
4.	Eat a lot of fatty foods	Eat salad and vegetables
5.	Skip breakfast	Eat fruit and yogurt for breakfast

1. _Emilia used to stay up until 2:00 a.m., but now she goes to bed at 10:00 p.m._

2. _____

3. _____

4. _____

5. _____

5 Write questions and answers about what Emilia used to do. Use the information in Exercise 4.

1. Emilia / stay up until 2:00 a.m.

   A _Did Emilia use to stay up until 2:00 a.m._____?

   B _____.

2. she / eat meat every day

   A _____?

   B _____.

3. she / go to the gym three times a week

   A _____?

   B _____.

Check your answers. See pages 136–137.

1 **Read and answer the questions. Then listen.**

TRACK 14

THREE **BENEFICIAL** HERBS

Many herbal plants are easy to grow. You can use them in cooking and to prevent illness. You can grow thyme, lavender, and mint in a garden or in your home.

Thyme is a small herbal plant. You can use it in cooking and as a medicine. The leaves are gray-green, and the flowers are usually purple, white, or pink. Many people use thyme to cook chicken and fish. You can also dry the leaves and make tea with them. Thyme tea with honey is very good for a cough or a sore throat.

Lavender is a popular garden plant with silver-green leaves and tiny purple flowers. The flowers have a beautiful smell. You can use the dried flowers to keep clothes and sheets fresh. You can use lavender when cooking meat, and you can make tea from the dried flowers for headaches. Using lavender may even keep blood pressure low. Some people use lavender oil in their bath to help them relax.

Mint is a beneficial plant that grows quickly. You can use the leaves in salads and with meat or fish. You can use the fresh or dried leaves to make tea. It helps with indigestion and upset stomachs. Add sugar to iced mint tea for a delicious summer drink.

Use thyme, lavender, and mint to stay healthy and prevent illness.

1. Which of the herbs in the article is good for treating indigestion?

_____

2. Which of the herbs in the article is good for treating headaches?

_____

3. Which of the herbs in the article is good for treating stomachaches?

_____

4. What illnesses in the article can thyme tea help treat?

_____

Check your answers. See page 137.

2 Complete the chart. Use the information in Exercise 1.

Name of plant	Use it to make . . .	Use it to cook . . .	Use it to treat . . .
Thyme	tea		
Lavender			
Mint			

3 Complete the sentences. Use the information in Exercise 1.

| digest | digestion | herbal | prevent | treat | treatment |

1. I'm having problems with my ___digestion___. I think I'll drink some mint tea.

2. Some people use thyme tea as a _____ for sore throats.

3. Lavender can help _____ high blood pressure.

4. You can use mint to make delicious _____ tea.

5. Mint can help you _____ your food.

6. Some people use lavender tea to _____ headaches.

4 Write *adjective*, *noun*, or *verb*.

1. digestive: ___adjective___

2. prevention: _____

3. treat: _____

4. herbs: _____

5. digest: _____

6. prevent: _____

7. treatment: _____

LESSON E Writing

1 Read about sage. Then answer the questions.

Sage is a popular herbal plant used for cooking and medicine. It is easy to grow in your garden. It has green-gray leaves and purple flowers. You can make tea from the leaves to treat sore throats and breathing problems. I also use it to add flavor to meat or vegetables. I sometimes use sage tea as a mouthwash, too.

1. What is sage used for? *cooking and medicine* _____

2. What does it look like? _____

3. What health problems can you treat with sage? _____

4. How can you use it in cooking? _____

5. How else can you use it? _____

2 Complete the paragraph. Use the information in the chart.

Plant name	rosemary
Grows	in the garden or in your home
Description	sharp, narrow leaves
Treats	headaches
Cooking uses	adds flavor to meat or oil

_____*Rosemary*_____ is my favorite herbal plant. It is widely used for
　　　1
cooking and medicine. It is easy to grow in your _____. It has
　　　　　　　　　　　　　　　　　　　　　　　2
_____. You can use the leaves to treat _____.
　　　3　　　　　　　　　　　　　　　　　　　　4
I also use it in cooking to _____.
　　　　　　　　　　　　　5

Check your answers. See page 137.

3 Read the chart. Answer the questions.

Plant name	aloe vera
History	people have used it for 6,000 years
Grows	in hot, dry places
Description	• long, spiky leaves • leaves have juice inside them
Treats	• burns • insect bites • dry skin
Used in	• skin creams and lotions • shampoos • soaps

1. Where does aloe vera grow? *in hot, dry places* _____

2. What kind of leaves does it have? _____

3. What problems can you treat with aloe vera? _____

4. What products have aloe vera in them? _____

4 Write a paragraph about aloe vera. Use the information in Exercise 3.

People have used aloe vera for thousands of years. _____

_____

_____

_____

_____

_____

_____

_____

_____

_____

1 Read the questions. Look at the form. Then fill in the correct answers.

Medical History Form

1. What is the reason for your visit?

Problem   Date problem began
_____allergies_____   _____3 weeks ago_____

2. Have you ever had any of the following?

☑ allergies	☐ back pain	☑ headaches	☑ high blood pressure
☐ arthritis	☐ chest pains	☐ heart attack	☑ high cholesterol
☑ asthma	☐ diabetes	☐ heart disease	☐ tuberculosis

3. Please list all medications, including vitamins and herbal supplements.
_____Vitamin C, garlic pills, and aspirin_____

4. List any other major illnesses, injuries, or surgeries you have had in the last year.

_____

The above information is correct to the best of my knowledge.

Signature _____Eva Hernandez_____   Date _____August 25, 2013_____

1. Eva went to the doctor because of _____.
   Ⓐ arthritis
   ● allergies
   Ⓒ diabetes
   Ⓓ back pain

2. Eva does not take _____.
   Ⓐ aspirin
   Ⓑ garlic pills
   Ⓒ Vitamin C
   Ⓓ Vitamin D

3. In the past, Eva has had _____.
   Ⓐ chest pains
   Ⓑ tuberculosis
   Ⓒ heart disease
   Ⓓ high cholesterol

4. In the past, Eva has not had _____.
   Ⓐ asthma
   Ⓑ headaches
   Ⓒ heart disease
   Ⓓ high blood pressure

Check your answers. See page 137.

2 Look at the pictures. Complete the indirect commands.

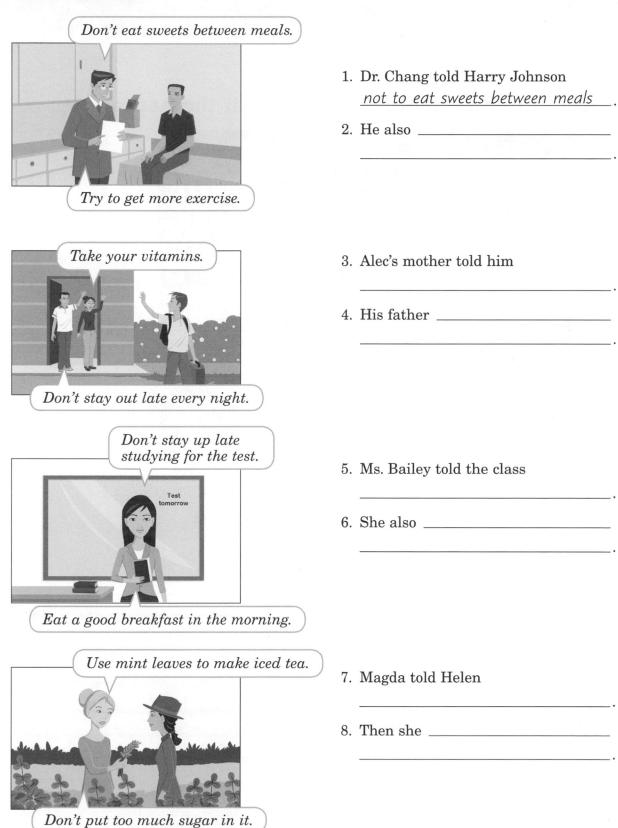

1. Dr. Chang told Harry Johnson
   not to eat sweets between meals .
2. He also _____
   _____ .

3. Alec's mother told him
   _____ .
4. His father _____
   _____ .

5. Ms. Bailey told the class
   _____ .
6. She also _____
   _____ .

7. Magda told Helen
   _____ .
8. Then she _____
   _____ .

LESSON A Listening

1 Read the ads. Match the ads with the sentences.

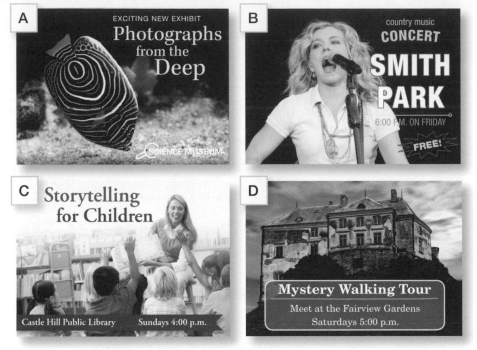

A EXCITING NEW EXHIBIT
Photographs from the Deep
SCIENCE MUSEUM

B country music CONCERT
SMITH PARK
6:00 P.M. ON FRIDAY
FREE!

C Storytelling for Children
Castle Hill Public Library   Sundays 4:00 p.m.

D Mystery Walking Tour
Meet at the Fairview Gardens
Saturdays 5:00 p.m.

1. Rick and Becky can't afford to spend a lot on entertainment. _B_

2. Bill and Margie want to get some exercise and be outside. _D_

3. Maria's daughter loves books. _C_

4. The weather is bad, so Lin wants to do something interesting indoors. _A_

2 Complete the sentences.

admission	afford	concerts	events	exhibits	storytelling

1. We usually check the newspaper for community _events_ .

2. I love music. I like going to rock _concerts_ .

3. We don't have any money. We can't _afford_ expensive tickets.

4. The garden tour is free. There is no _admission_ fee.

5. My children love stories. They love listening to _storytelling_ at the library.

6. My wife loves art. She often goes to art _exhibits_ .

Check your answers. See page 137.

3 Read and circle the correct answers. Then listen.

TRACK 15

A Yan, do you have any plans for Saturday?

B No, Lin, not yet.

A There's a free concert in the park on Saturday afternoon. Do you want to go?

B That sounds good. What time does it start?

A It starts at 3:00. And there's a new art exhibit at the museum.

B What time does the museum open?

A 10:00. And it's free admission.

B OK. Let's meet at the museum at 11:00. We'll have lunch in the museum café, and then we'll go to the concert.

1. Yan and Lin are _____.
   a. going shopping
   b. discussing music
   c. choosing a good restaurant
   d. planning their weekend

2. They are going to go to _____.
   a. a park and a concert
   b. a park and a movie
   c. an art exhibit and a concert
   d. an art exhibit and a movie

3. First, Yan and Lin will _____.
   a. walk in the park
   b. eat lunch at a café
   c. go to a free concert
   d. meet at an art museum

4. The museum opens at _____.
   a. 9:00 a.m.
   b. 10:00 a.m.
   c. 11:00 a.m.
   d. 3:00 p.m.

5. Which statement is true?
   a. The concert tickets are not cheap.
   b. There is no admission fee for the concert.
   c. Admission to the museum is not free.
   d. Admission to the museum is expensive.

6. Yan and Lin will spend _____.
   a. no money at all
   b. no money on food
   c. some money on food
   d. some money on entertainment

4 What are Leo and Noriko going to do? Listen and check.

TRACK 16

☐ go to a movie   ☐ go out for dinner

☐ go to a museum   ☐ go out for coffee

LESSON B Verbs + infinitives

Study the chart and explanation on page 127.

1 Complete the sentences. Use the infinitive. Then listen.

TRACK 17

| come home | eat | go | meet | see | take |

A Nina, where have you decided _____*to go*_____ this afternoon?
                                                       1

B I'm going to the art museum with my friend Gabe.

A What do you want _to see_ ?
                                                   2

B There's a new exhibit on American paintings.

A Where have you agreed _to meet_ Gabe?
                                                   3

B Outside the art museum at 1:00.

A Where do you plan _to eat_ ?
                                                   4

B We'll eat lunch at home.

A Can you afford _to take_ a taxi?
                                                   5

B No, we'll take the subway.

A What time do you expect _to come home_ ?
                                                   6

B I should be home before 6:00.

2 Complete the sentences. Use the infinitive.

1. Nina doesn't _____*want to ride*_____ her bike this afternoon.
                                (want / ride)

2. She _plans to eat_ at home.
                     (plan / eat)

3. She _intends to meet_ Gabe at the museum.
                     (intend / meet)

4. She doesn't _need to take_ a taxi.
                     (need / take)

5. She _expects to be_ home by 6:00.
                     (expects / be)

6. She _would like to buy_ something from the gift shop.
                     (would like / buy)

7. She _hopes to find_ something that is not too expensive.
                     (hope / find)

Check your answers. See page 137.

46 Novels Then and Now

Do you like to read novels? Many people do. Would it surprise you to know that novels are a <u>rather</u> new thing? They didn't exist until a few hundred years ago.

Some people say that the first novel was Cervantes' *Don Quixote* (kee HO tay). This Spanish story of a <u>knight</u> and his servant was written in the early 1600s. The two go from one adventure to another. The book follows their progress.

Modern novels usually have a more continuous story than *Don Quixote*. And their characters are more realistic. Novels of this sort did not appear until about 1740. At that time English writer Samuel Richardson published *Pamela*. This novel is about a young servant woman. The son of her employer tries to seduce her, but she does not give in. After *Pamela* many other novels were quickly published. Henry Fielding's *Tom Jones* tells of a young man who does not know who his parents are. His adventures paint a clear picture of English life at that time. Another early novel is *Robinson Crusoe* by Daniel Dafoe. It is about a man alone on a desert island.

Today there are many kinds of novels to choose from. In detective novels the hero is an investigator who solves a crime. Some of the earliest stories of this type were about Sherlock Holmes. But now there are many others. Author P. D. James writes about Adam Dalgleish. John D. McDonald wrote about Travis McGee.

Another type is the historical novel. In this kind of novel, made-up characters are placed in a real historical setting. It may be the Civil War, as in Margaret Mitchell's *Gone with the Wind*. It may even be the Stone Age.

Especially popular are Gothic novels. These are tales of terror with <u>eerie</u> settings and moods. A well-known modern Gothic writer is Stephen King.

Main Idea 1

	Answer	Score
Mark the *main idea*	M	15
Mark the statement that is *too broad*	B	5
Mark the statement that is *too narrow*	N	5

a. Some early detective novels were about Sherlock Holmes. N | ____

b. Reading novels is a popular form of entertainment. B | ____

c. Novels have developed from the 1600s to the present time. M | ____

Add your scores and on the grap

Subject Matter	**2**	Another good title for this passage would be	

☑ a. What Made English Novels Popular.

☑ b. A Short History of the Novel.

☐ c. Types of Modern Novels.

☐ d. The First Novel.

_____

Supporting Details	**3**	Novels set in an atmosphere filled with fear and terror are called

☐ a. historical novels.

☐ b. adventure novels.

☐ c. detective novels.

☑ d. Gothic novels.

_____

Conclusion	**4**	We can conclude from this passage that Travis McGee was

☑ a. a character who investigated crimes.

☐ b. the hero in *Gone with the Wind.*

☑ c. a real person.

☐ d. a character similar to Tom Jones.

_____

Clarifying Devices	**5**	The author presents information in this passage

☑ a. from the past to the present.

☐ b. from the present to the past.

☑ c. in order of importance.

☐ d. by describing the setting of each novel.

_____

Vocabulary in Context	**6**	Eerie means

☑ a. spooky.

☑ b. exciting.

☐ c. colorful.

☐ d. noisy.

_____

Score

15

5

5

_____

_____

_____

Add your scores for questions 1–6. Enter the total here and on the graph on page 215.   Total Score   _____

3 Rewrite the sentences. Use the verb in parentheses and an infinitive.

1. Tony will visit his family every year. (promise)
   Tony promises to visit his family every year.

2. Lee will finish work early tonight. (expect)
   Lee expects to work early tonight.

3. I'll go to Florida this winter. (plan)
   _____

4. Shin will buy some concert tickets tomorrow. (intend)
   _____

5. We will visit our daughter in California next month. (hope)
   _____

6. Paul will not go to the beach this weekend. (refuse)
   _____

7. I will meet my friends on my birthday. (want)
   _____

8. I will take a trip with my family next year. (would like)
   _____

4 Complete the sentences about Chris's goals.

CHRIS'S GOALS

January	February	March	April	May	June
Watch less TV	Go to an art museum	Visit relatives more often	Walk to work every day	Give up desserts	Buy organic vegetables

1. (plan) In January, *Chris plans to watch less TV* .
2. (intend) In February, _____ .
3. (want) In March, _____ .
4. (plan) In April, _____ .
5. (would like) In May, _____ .
6. (hope) In June, _____ .

Check your answers. See page 137.

LESSON C Present perfect

Study the list of irregular verbs on page 128.

1 Complete the sentences. Use the present perfect.

1. Have Sue and Martin ____seen____ that movie already?
   (see)

2. Has Tim _____ dinner yet?
   (make)

3. We haven't _____ the newspaper yet.
   (read)

4. Have you _____ the credit card bill already?
   (pay)

5. My brother has already _____ his tickct.
   (buy)

6. Have the children _____ their homework yet?
   (do)

2 Complete the sentences. Use *already* or *yet*.

1. It's 8:00 p.m.
   The violin concert ____hasn't started yet____.
   (start)

2. It's 6:30 p.m.
   The coffee shop _____.
   (close)

3. It's 7:00 p.m.
   The movie _____.
   (end)

4. It's 9:00 a.m.
   The museum _____.
   (open)

Violin Concert Tonight
8:30 p.m.

Open for tea and coffee
11:00 a.m. to 6:00 p.m.

Movie matinee special
at 5:00 p.m.
Running time: 1 hour 40 minutes

Museum Hours:
Mon.–Sat.
10:00 a.m. to 6:00 p.m.
Closed Sunday

Check your answers. See page 137.

3 Max and Maria are planning a birthday party. Complete the sentences and answer the questions.

TO DO

Max	Maria	Max and Maria
bring my CDs ✓	invite friends ✓	set up tables and chairs
get a present	bake a cake	put up decorations ✓
buy drinks ✓		

1. ___Has___ Max ___brought___ his CDs yet?   ___Yes, he has.___

2. _____ Maria _____ their friends yet?   _____

3. _____ Max _____ a present yet?   _____

4. _____ Maria _____ a cake yet?   _____

5. _____ Max _____ drinks yet?   _____

6. _____ Max and Maria _____ decorations yet?   _____

7. _____ Max and Maria _____ the tables and chairs yet?   _____

4 Each of the sentences below is missing a word. Write the sentences with the missing word in parentheses.

1. We haven't gone to the park. (yet)

   We haven't gone to the park yet.

2. Our favorite TV show hasn't yet. (started)

   _____

3. Have bought tickets for the fund-raiser yet? (you)

   _____

4. They eaten lunch yet. (haven't)

   _____

5. Ivan and Alex already been to that restaurant. (have)

   _____

6. Julie visited the art exhibit yet? (has)

   _____

Check your answers. See page 137.   **UNIT 5 59**

1 Scan the article. Circle *T* (True) or *F* (False). Then listen and read.

TRACK 18

1. Four hundred people attended this superb performance.	T	(F)
2. The show started at 7:00 p.m. with Alvarez's band.	T	F
3. Alvarez performed four new songs.	T	F
4. Some people waited in line for 30 minutes to buy a soda.	T	F
5. There was no food available after 9:00 p.m.	T	F
6. Alvarez performed until 11:00 p.m.	T	F
7. Alvarez will perform four more times.	T	F

RUDY ALVAREZ at the Park Theater

by Mike Clark

A huge crowd gathered to see the rock musician Rudy Alvarez perform at the Park Theater on Saturday night. Over 500 people attended this superb event.

The show started at 7:00 p.m. with a salsa band. The band's music was unremarkable, and the lead singer did not sing well at all. It was irritating, and everyone wanted Alvarez to come on stage. Finally, the salsa band finished, and Alvarez came on stage at 8:30 p.m. The versatile artist performed his most popular songs and five new songs. The audience went wild! Everyone danced and sang along, and children climbed onto the stage and started dancing.

One negative side to the event was that the lines were long for refreshments. The waiting time was really excessive. Some people waited in line for 30 minutes to buy a soda, and there was no food available after 9:00 p.m. I also expected Alvarez to perform until about 11:00 p.m., but the show ended at 10:30 because of a serious problem with the sound system. We didn't get to hear Alvarez sing his most famous song, "Missing You."

Alvarez will give three more performances at the Park Theater and one additional performance at the Grand Theater. If you haven't attended one of his shows yet, don't miss your chance!

Check your answers. See page 137.

2 Circle the correct answers. Use the information in Exercise 1.

1. Why did the concert finish early?
   a. The weather was bad.
   b. The lines were too long.
   c. The audience was too wild.
   d. The sound system wasn't working properly.

2. What word did Mike Clark use to describe the salsa band?
   a. popular
   b. versatile
   c. excessive
   d. unremarkable

3. What word did Mike Clark use to describe Alvarez?
   a. superb
   b. versatile
   c. irritating
   d. available

4. Which statement is true?
   a. The audience liked the salsa band.
   b. The audience didn't sing any of the songs.
   c. Alvarez played his least popular songs.
   d. Alvarez played his most popular songs.

5. What was one negative thing about the concert?
   a. Children tried to get on stage.
   b. There wasn't enough food.
   c. Alvarez's music was unremarkable.
   d. Alvarez sang too many new songs.

3 Look at the bold words. Write the sentences. Use words from the box with a similar meaning.

crowd	excessive	missed	musicians	superb	unremarkable

1. We **didn't go** to the concert.   We missed the concert.

2. The concert was **excellent**.   _____

3. There was a **large group of people**.   _____

4. The waiting time was **too long**.   _____

5. There were five **people playing drums**.   _____

6. The stage was **not interesting**.   _____

Check your answers. See page 137.

LESSON E Writing

1 Complete the word maps.

amazing	fabulous	irritating	superb
excessive	incredible	ominous	unremarkable

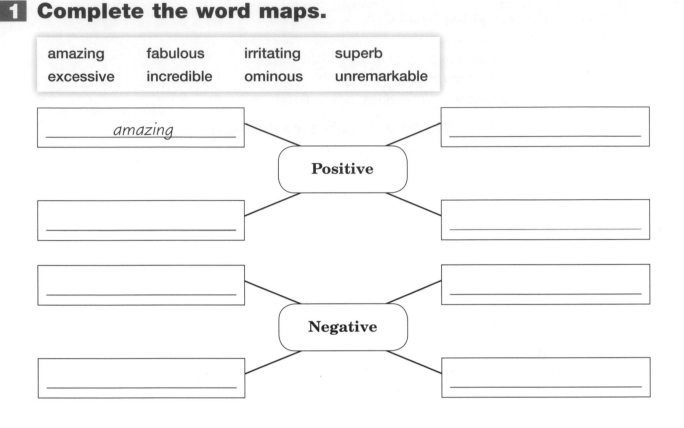

amazing

Positive

Negative

2 Read the postcard. Circle three positive adjectives. Underline three negative adjectives.

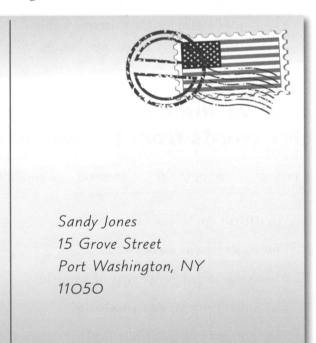

Hi Sandy,
     We had a (fabulous) time at
the Rudy Alvarez concert last night.
He is such an incredible musician.
First, there was a terrible salsa band,
and the lead singer was irritating.
But then Alvarez came on stage, and
his songs were amazing. Some of his
new songs were unremarkable, but he
played all of his popular old ones. We
danced for hours! I hope you can come
with us to the next show!
     Miss you!
     Rita

Sandy Jones
15 Grove Street
Port Washington, NY
11050

Check your answers. See page 137.

3 Match the sentence parts. Write *N* for negative information and *P* for positive information.

1. _N_ The musicians were irritating because   a. we couldn't see very well.

2. ____ Our seats were in the back, so   b. they couldn't sing.

3. ____ The weather was bad, and   c. we danced all night.

4. ____ The music was awesome, and   d. we couldn't hear anything.

5. ____ The music wasn't loud enough, and   e. we were cold.

4 Read Bill's notes about a jazz concert. Write an e-mail about the concert. Use positive and negative information.

Jazz Harmony Concert

POSITIVE	NEGATIVE
concert started on time	music wasn't loud enough
fabulous seats	concert hall was too big
band played for a long time	tickets too expensive
band played awesome new songs	got home very late

To: ralph@cup.org
From: bill@cup.org
Subject: Jazz Harmony Concert

Hi Ralph,

I went to the Jazz Harmony concert last week.

_____

_____

_____

_____

_____

_____

_____

_____

LESSON F Another view

1 **Read the questions. Look at the announcements. Then fill in the correct answers.**

International Fair

Food and music from 20 different countries. Sat. 10:00 a.m. to 5:00 p.m., Sun. 10:00 a.m. to 3:00 p.m. at the Community Center. Free admission.

Animal Movies

Educational movies – fun for children and adults. Wednesday, September 19th, at 5:00 p.m. East Riverside Public Library. No admission fee.

Nature Tour

Have you joined the Friends of Mission Park yet? Come for an easy guided walk around the park on Sunday. Meet at the Information Center at noon. Tickets: $3.00 for adults, $2.00 for children.

Community Barbecue

Have you seen your friends and neighbors lately? Then join us for burgers and all the fixin's. This Sunday, 11:00 to 3:00. All you can eat meal tickets: $7.00.

1. At which event can you get some exercise?
   ● Nature Tour
   Ⓑ Animal Movies
   Ⓒ International Fair
   Ⓓ Community Barbecue

2. Which event starts at 10:00 a.m. on Sunday?
   Ⓐ Nature Tour
   Ⓑ Animal Movies
   Ⓒ International Fair
   Ⓓ Community Barbecue

3. Which event is the most expensive?
   Ⓐ Nature Tour
   Ⓑ Animal Movies
   Ⓒ International Fair
   Ⓓ Community Barbecue

4. Which events are free?
   Ⓐ International Fair and Nature Tour
   Ⓑ Nature Tour and Animal Movies
   Ⓒ Animal Movies and International Fair
   Ⓓ Community Barbecue and Nature Tour

5. Which event does not take place on a weekend?
   Ⓐ Nature Tour
   Ⓑ Animal Movies
   Ⓒ International Fair
   Ⓓ Community Barbecue

6. At which events can you eat food?
   Ⓐ Community Barbecue and Nature Tour
   Ⓑ Animal Movies and Community Barbecue
   Ⓒ International Fair and Nature Tour
   Ⓓ Community Barbecue and International Fair

Check your answers. See page 137.

2 Complete the sentences with an infinitive or a gerund.

1. I've already finished ___reading___ the story.
   (read)

2. We've decided _____ on the garden tour.
   (go)

3. Rick promised _____ the tickets.
   (buy)

4. Mayuko dislikes _____ late for concerts.
   (be)

5. Do you enjoy _____ to country music?
   (listen)

6. Alan refused _____ the scary movie.
   (see)

7. We usually avoid _____ in that park at night.
   (walk)

8. They wanted _____ at the library, but it was closed.
   (study)

3 Write new sentences with an infinitive or a gerund when possible. If not possible, put an ✗ in the box.

1. Betty prefers to go to crafts fairs, not to the mall.

   ☐ _Betty prefers going to crafts fairs, not to the mall._

2 The guide suggested going on the historic walking tour.

   ✗ _____

3. The lights went out, but the musicians continued playing.

   ☐ _____

4. I avoided going to the dentist, and now my tooth hurts.

   ☐ _____

5. I started reading the book last night.

   ☐ _____

6. Why do you dislike watching tennis on TV?

   ☐ _____

7. The band plans to give another concert tomorrow.

   ☐ _____

8. Raul hates to drive in the city during rush hour.

   ☐ _____

LESSON **A** Listening

1 Complete the sentences.

chores	due	prioritize	tasks
deadline	impatient	procrastinating	

1. One of my _____chores_____ is to take out the trash.

2. The _____ for my project is tomorrow.

3. I have another project _____ next week.

4. You have to make a to-do list of _____ in order of importance.

5. Do your homework now and stop _____!

6. I have too many things to do this weekend. I need to

   _____ them.

7. Please don't be so _____! Your food will be ready soon.

2 Read and complete Olivia's journal entry. Then listen.

TRACK 19

chores	due	impatient	prioritize	procrastinating	to-do list

I have too many things to do today. My friends are coming over for dinner tonight.

I need to make a _____to-do list_____ and stop _____ . I have
                          1   2

to buy food for dinner. I have some _____ to do around the house,
                                            3

and I also have to finish my homework. It's _____ tomorrow.
                                                    4

Now I need to _____ the tasks on my list. First, I want to do the
                      5

shopping because it is the most important. Next, I'll cook the food. My friends might

get _____ if they have to wait for dinner. Then, I'll clean up the
           6

house. Will I have time to do my homework before they arrive? Probably not.

Check your answers. See page 138.

3 Circle the correct answers. Use the information in Exercise 2.

1. What is Olivia's problem?
   a. She has too many things to do.
   b. She has too much homework.
   c. She doesn't want to prioritize.
   d. She doesn't have enough work to do.

2. Olivia needs to stop _____.
   a. cooking
   b. procrastinating
   c. doing chores
   d. doing her homework

3. When Olivia *prioritizes*, she'll do _____.
   a. some of her tasks
   b. the most difficult tasks later
   c. the most important tasks first
   d. all of the tasks as quickly as possible

4. What will she do before she cooks?
   a. clean up
   b. go shopping
   c. take out the trash
   d. finish her homework

5. When friends are *impatient*, they are not willing to _____.
   a. eat
   b. wait
   c. prioritize
   d. procrastinate

6. When you don't *have time*, you are too _____.
   a. busy
   b. late
   c. upset
   d. tired

4 Match.

1. do _b_
2. make _____
3. take out _____
4. prioritize _____
5. be _____

a. impatient
b. homework
c. tasks
d. the trash
e. a to-do list

5 Listen. Then check (✓) two true statements.

TRACK 20

☐ Thomas makes to-do lists at work.
☐ Alicia has learned to manage her time.
☐ Thomas often procrastinates.
☐ Alicia doesn't have time to go to the gym.

LESSON B Adverb clauses

Study the explanation on page 133.

1 Make sentences. Match the sentence parts.

1. When I need to concentrate, _b_
2. When I feel tired, _____
3. When I have a deadline, _____
4. When I don't understand a grammar question, _____
5. When I don't understand a word, _____
6. When I have many tasks to do, _____

a. I don't procrastinate.
b. I turn off the TV.
c. I use a dictionary.
d. I make a to-do list.
e. I take a break.
f. I ask my teacher.

2 Combine the sentences. Use *when*.

1. Parvana has a lot of homework. She makes a to-do list of her tasks.

   When _____.

2. She wants to concentrate. She goes to the library.

   When _____, _____.

3. She looks at the clock. She starts her work.

   _____ when _____.

4. She finishes a task. She checks it off her to-do list.

   When _____, _____.

5. She takes a short break. She feels tired.

   _____ when _____.

6. She doesn't hand in her homework on time. Her teacher is upset.

   When _____, _____.

7. She eats a snack. She feels hungry.

   _____ when _____.

8. She needs to focus. She doesn't answer the phone.

   When _____, _____.

9. She does the difficult tasks first. She has a lot of work to do.

   _____ when _____.

10. She has a deadline. She doesn't procrastinate.

    When _____, _____.

Check your answers. See page 138.

3 Read the sentences. Add commas if necessary. Write *no comma* if you do not need a comma.

1. When I finish my homework I take a break. _____

2. Than procrastinates when he doesn't want to do his homework. _____

3. Suzanna uses a dictionary when she reads the newspaper. _____

4. When we don't hand in our homework our teacher is very upset. _____

5. When I have a deadline I stay up late. _____

6. Sushila doesn't like to work when she is tired. _____

4 Write questions. Then write the answers.

I ask my teacher.	I procrastinate.	I study my notes.
I go to the library.	I rest.	I take a break.

1. (do / finish a difficult task)

   A What *do you do when you finish a difficult task* _____?

   B *I take a break* _____.

2. (do / need to concentrate)

   A What _____?

   B _____.

3. (do / don't understand the homework)

   A What _____?

   B _____.

4. (do / have a quiz or test)

   A What _____?

   B _____.

5. (do / feel tired)

   A What _____?

   B _____.

6. (do / don't want to work)

   A What _____?

   B _____.

Check your answers. See page 138.

LESSON C Adverb clauses

Study the explanation on page 133.

1 Complete the sentences. Use *after*.

Mannie's morning schedule

5:30 wake up
5:45 get dressed
6:00 eat breakfast
6:30 work out
7:15 take a shower
8:00 go to work

1. Mannie gets dressed _____ *after he wakes up* _____.

2. Mannie eats breakfast _____.

3. Mannie works out _____.

4. Mannie takes a shower _____.

5. Mannie goes to work _____.

2 Write sentences. Use *before*.

Janet's evening schedule

5:30 get home
6:00 eat dinner
7:00 walk the dog
8:00 watch TV
9:00 read a book
9:30 go to bed

1. get home / eat dinner

   Janet gets home before she eats dinner. _____

2. eat dinner / walk the dog

   _____

3. walk the dog / watch TV

   _____

4. watch TV / read a book

   _____

Check your answers. See page 138.

3 Write questions. Then write the answers. Use the information in Exercises 1 and 2.

1. Mannie / do / before / eat breakfast

   A What *does Mannie do before he eats breakfast* _____?

   B *He gets dressed.* _____

2. Mannie / do / before / work out

   A What _____?

   B _____

3. Mannie / do / before / go to work

   A What _____?

   B _____

4. Janet / do / after / get home

   A What _____?

   B _____

5. Janet / do / after / watch TV

   A What _____?

   B _____

6. Janet / do / after / read a book

   A What _____?

   B _____

4 Underline the activity that happens first. Circle the activity that happens second.

1. (I watch TV) after I have dinner.

2. Before Sandy goes to work, she buys a newspaper.

3. Ivana goes to school after she finishes work.

4. After Simon finishes his homework, he takes a break.

5. They usually go swimming after they go to the park.

6. Before you go out, you need to take out the trash.

7. Melanie puts on makeup after she takes a shower.

8. Alan washes the dishes before he goes to bed.

Check your answers. See page 138.

LESSON D Reading

1 Read and circle the correct answers. Then listen.

Feature Story

Personal Rules about Time

Everyone has his or her own personal rules about time. These rules depend on the personality of the person as well as on the culture of the country.

Some individuals – no matter where they are from – have very strict rules about time. They like to keep a schedule. They are always early for meetings. When they catch a train, they arrive at the station 30 minutes before the train leaves. When they go to a party, they are often the first guests to arrive. It is sometimes difficult for these people to understand why their co-workers and friends cannot be on time. They get angry when their friends are late.

Other people are not very strict about time – even in places like the United States, Canada, and England, where punctuality is generally considered to be very important. They don't think keeping a schedule is the most important thing. For example, they are sometimes late for work, they often miss trains and buses, and they arrive at a party one or two hours after the party has started. They don't understand why other people get upset when they are late. On the other hand, these people do not get impatient when their friends are late!

1. This article talks about two different _____ .
   a. how to keep a schedule
   b. why punctuality is important
   c. ways of thinking about time
   d. types of social and business events

2. When people are strict about time, they _____ .
   a. keep a schedule
   b. come from special countries
   c. are always late for appointments
   d. are good and understanding friends

3. When people are not strict about time, they are _____ .
   a. never late
   b. not punctual
   c. schedule keepers
   d. always impatient

4. According to the article, people should _____ .
   a. always be on time
   b. have personal rules about time
   c. understand their friends
   d. understand different rules about time

Check your answers. See page 138.

2 Complete the sentences.

| impatient | impolite | irresponsible | punctuality | uncommon |

1. In Canada, it is ___impolite___ to arrive at a dinner party more than 10 minutes late.

2. People who are strict about time get _____ when their friends are late.

3. In England, _____ is an unspoken rule. Being on time is important.

4. It is _____ to be late for a job interview in the United States.

5. In Brazil, it is not _____ for guests to arrive two hours after a social event begins.

3 Rewrite the sentences. Write the bold words with the prefixes *un-*, *dis-*, *ir-*, or *im-*.

1. It is **not common** to miss a plane.
   It is uncommon to miss a plane.

2. It is **not polite** to be late.
   _____

3. It is **not usual** to be early for a party.
   _____

4. He is **not patient**.
   _____

5. They are **not responsible**.
   _____

6. She is **not organized**.
   _____

4 Write the opposites.

1. unlucky   _lucky_
2. impossible   _____
3. dishonest   _____
4. unfriendly   _____
5. unkind   _____
6. irrational   _____

Check your answers. See page 138.

1 Read the paragraph. Then answer the questions.

An Organized Student

Nita is a very organized person. For example, she keeps all of her class notes in one binder with different sections. Each section has a label. She also writes all of her homework assignments and due dates in a special notebook. Before she goes home, she checks her bag carefully. She makes sure she has all the books she needs. After she gets home, she has dinner. Then she plans how much time she will need for each assignment. She makes a list of tasks and crosses them out when she finishes them. When she feels tired, she takes a short break. In summary, Nita is an organized person and a successful student.

1. What is the topic sentence?

   Nita is a very organized person.

2. What is the first example?

   _____

3. What is the second example?

   _____

4. Which words signal the conclusion?

   _____

2 Answer the questions. Use the information in Exercise 1.

1. Why doesn't Nita forget the due dates of her assignments?

   She writes all her homework assignments and the due dates in a special notebook.

2. Where does she keep her notes?

   _____

3. What does she do before she goes home?

   _____

4. What does she plan after dinner?

   _____

5. What does she do when she feels tired?

   _____

Check your answers. See page 138.

3 **Write the sentences in the correct order to make a paragraph.**

> ### An Impatient Boss
>
> She is also not a good listener, and she often interrupts.
>
> For example, she often gets angry when you are three minutes late.
>
> Finally, she is always in a hurry and never has enough time.
>
> My boss Frida is a very impatient person.
>
> In conclusion, Frida is a very impatient person, and it is difficult to work for her.

My boss Frida is a very impatient person.

_____

_____

_____

_____

4 **Write a short paragraph about Paula. Include a topic sentence, examples to support your topic sentence, and a signal before your conclusion.**

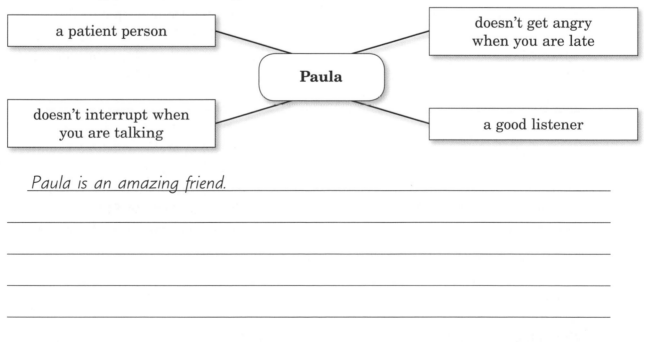

a patient person

doesn't get angry when you are late

Paula

doesn't interrupt when you are talking

a good listener

Paula is an amazing friend.

_____

_____

_____

_____

Check your answers. See page 138.

LESSON F Another view

1 **Read the questions. Look at the pie chart. Then fill in the correct answers.**

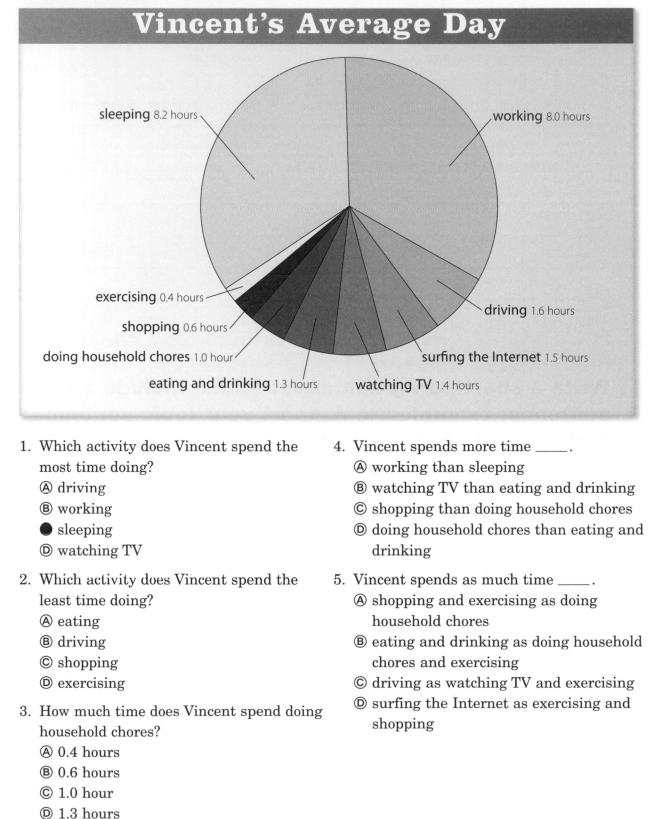

Vincent's Average Day

- sleeping 8.2 hours
- working 8.0 hours
- exercising 0.4 hours
- shopping 0.6 hours
- doing household chores 1.0 hour
- eating and drinking 1.3 hours
- watching TV 1.4 hours
- surfing the Internet 1.5 hours
- driving 1.6 hours

1. Which activity does Vincent spend the most time doing?
   - Ⓐ driving
   - Ⓑ working
   - ● sleeping
   - Ⓓ watching TV

2. Which activity does Vincent spend the least time doing?
   - Ⓐ eating
   - Ⓑ driving
   - Ⓒ shopping
   - Ⓓ exercising

3. How much time does Vincent spend doing household chores?
   - Ⓐ 0.4 hours
   - Ⓑ 0.6 hours
   - Ⓒ 1.0 hour
   - Ⓓ 1.3 hours

4. Vincent spends more time _____.
   - Ⓐ working than sleeping
   - Ⓑ watching TV than eating and drinking
   - Ⓒ shopping than doing household chores
   - Ⓓ doing household chores than eating and drinking

5. Vincent spends as much time _____.
   - Ⓐ shopping and exercising as doing household chores
   - Ⓑ eating and drinking as doing household chores and exercising
   - Ⓒ driving as watching TV and exercising
   - Ⓓ surfing the Internet as exercising and shopping

Check your answers. See page 138.

2 Circle the correct word.

1. **A** Have you taken out the trash?

   B No, I haven't taken (it)/ **one** out yet.

2. **A** Has Charlene done her chores yet?

   B Yes, she has. She's done **any** / **them** already.

3. **A** Are there any science programs on TV tonight?

   B Yes, there's **one** / **some** on at 8:00 on channel 10.

4. **A** Have you seen my math book?

   B Yes, **one's** / **it's** on the table.

5. **A** Do you have any questions about the reading?

   B Yes, I have **some** / **any**.

6. **A** Are there any tickets for the concert?

   B Yes. Do you want to buy **it** / **one**?

3 Write true answers to the questions. Use *one*, *it*, or *them* in your answers.

1. Have you ever memorized a song?

   _Yes, I've memorized one_____ Or _No, I haven't memorized one._

2. Have you seen the movie *Casablanca*?

   _____

3. Have you ever made a to-do list?

   _____

4. Did you circle the correct answers in Exercise 2?

   _____

5. Do you have a blue pencil in your bag?

   _____

6. Do you ever visit friends on the weekend?

   _____

LESSON A Listening

1 Read and circle the correct answers. Then listen.

TRACK 22

SOFIA Do you use your credit card a lot?

JACKIE Yes. All the time! I have four cards.

SOFIA Really? Isn't it difficult to pay them off? The interest rates are so high!

JACKIE I never charge more than $100 on each card.

SOFIA I'm thinking about buying a new refrigerator, but I can't afford it.

JACKIE Why don't you buy it on credit? You can pay for it later.

SOFIA I don't want to get into debt. We already have to pay off our car loan.

JACKIE Maybe you could look in the newspaper or online and find a used refrigerator.

SOFIA That's a good idea.

1. Sofia wants to buy a refrigerator. What is the problem?
   a. She doesn't have a car.
   b. She doesn't have any credit.
   c. She doesn't have a credit card.
   d. She doesn't have enough money.

2. What does Jackie think Sofia should do?
   a. take out a loan
   b. get a new credit card
   c. pay off her car loan
   d. buy a used refrigerator

3. Which statement is true?
   a. Sofia wants a new credit card.
   b. Sofia never borrows money.
   c. Sofia is worried about getting into debt.
   d. Sofia needs to borrow money for her car loan.

4. Which statement is true?
   a. Jackie never uses a credit card.
   b. Jackie has more than one credit card.
   c. Jackie uses her credit card every day.
   d. Jackie spends too much on her credit card.

Check your answers. See page 139.

2 Complete the sentences.

| afford | balance | cash | credit | interest | pay off |

1. That car costs $30,000. We can't _____ it.

2. I'll buy the refrigerator on _____. I don't want to use my savings.

3. You should pay _____ for food. Don't use your credit card.

4. The _____ rate for the loan is too high.

5. If we _____ the loan in six months, there's no interest.

6. At the end of the month, the _____ in my bank account is usually low!

3 Solve the problems.

1. Su-lin and Chung-hee have a balance of $28,000.00 in their savings account. They want to buy a new car that costs $30,500.00. If they use all the money in their savings account, how much do they need to borrow to buy the new car? _____

Cost of new car: $30,500.00
Balance in savings account: -$28,000.00
Money they need to borrow: $2,500.00

2. Suzanne and Pete have a balance of $950.00 in their savings account. They want to buy a new refrigerator. It costs $1,200.00. If they use all the money in their savings account, how much do they need to borrow? _____

3. Dora and Julian have saved $1,500.00. They want to buy a television. It costs $1,200.00. They also need a new washing machine. It costs $800.00. If they use all their savings, how much do they need to borrow to buy the TV and the washing machine? _____

4 Listen. Then circle the correct amounts.

TRACK 23

1. The price of the first TV with the taxes and installation is about **$2,000 / $2,500**.

2. The interest rate on the loan for the TV is **24 / 36** percent.

3. The monthly payment on the TV loan would be almost **$36 / $100**.

4. The smaller TV costs only **$550 / $1,550**.

Check your answers. See page 139.   UNIT 7 **79**

LESSON B Modals

Study the chart on page 130.

1 Match the problems with the suggestions.

1. I can't afford gas for my car. _b_
2. My credit card bills are too high. ____
3. I need to find a job. ____
4. I can't afford a new computer. ____
5. My rent is too expensive. ____
6. My cell phone bill is too high. ____

a. You could use e-mail instead.
b. You could take the bus.
c. You could find a cheaper apartment.
d. You could look at an online job site.
e. You could talk to a debt counselor.
f. You could use your credit card.

2 Circle the correct form of the verb.

1. You should (buy) / buying a new car.
2. How about take / taking out a loan?
3. You could use / using a credit card.
4. Why don't you talk / talking to a debt counselor?
5. You should apply / applying for a scholarship.
6. How about look / looking in the newspaper?

3 Complete the sentences. Use could or should.

1. **A** I don't have enough money at the end of each month.
   Do you have any advice?

   B You ___should___ try to save a little each month.

2. **A** Where do you suggest I buy a new camera?

   B You _____ find one online, or you could go to the mall.

3. **A** I don't know how to apply for college. Can you give me any advice?

   B You _____ talk to a counselor.

4. **A** My tooth hurts. What should I do?

   B You _____ go to the dentist.

5. **A** Can you suggest a good place to go on vacation?

   B You _____ go to Hawaii or maybe Las Vegas.

6. **A** I want to get a good grade on my test. What should I do?

   B You _____ study hard this weekend.

Check your answers. See page 139.

4 Complete the sentences. Use an expression in the box.

buy a new one	looking for a cheaper plan	using your credit card
buy a used one	open a savings account	walking more often

1. **A** I don't have enough cash to pay for the tickets. What should I do?

   B How about _____ *using your credit card* _____?

2. **A** We need a car, but we can't afford to buy a new one.

   B You could _____.

3. **A** This sweater looks old.

   B You should _____.

4. **A** The price of gas is going up to $5.00 a gallon. What am I going to do?

   B You could start _____.

5. **A** I'm spending too much money on cell phone calls. Do you have any suggestions?

   B How about _____?

6. **A** I got a great bonus at work. What should I do with the money?

   B Why don't you _____?

5 Complete the sentences. Use *should* and the verbs in the box.

buy	do	make	tell	wear

1. **A** We don't have plans this weekend. What _____ *should we do* _____?

   B I don't know. Maybe we could go to the movies.

2. **A** I didn't finish the homework. What _____ my teacher?

   B You should tell your teacher the truth. You didn't have enough time.

3. **A** I'm going shopping tomorrow. What _____?

   B I think you should get a new pair of pants.

4. **A** I want to make a special dinner tonight. What _____?

   B Well, I like fish.

5. **A** I don't have any nice clothes for the party. What _____?

   B You should borrow my black jacket.

Check your answers. See page 139.

LESSON C Gerunds after prepositions

Study the chart and explanation on page 126.

1 Write the gerund form of each verb.

1. apply   *applying*
2. be   _____
3. buy   _____
4. find   _____
5. get   _____
6. lend   _____

7. lose   _____
8. make   _____
9. open   _____
10. pay   _____
11. study   _____
12. wait   _____

2 Complete the sentences. Use words from Exercise 1.

1. He is tired of _____*waiting*_____ .

2. She is happy about _____ a new car.

3. He is interested in _____ for a loan.

4. She is thinking about _____ a savings account.

5. He is excited about _____ auto mechanics.

6. She is afraid of _____ into debt.

Check your answers. See page 139.

3 Circle the correct preposition.

1. Martina is worried **(about)**/ **of** paying her bills.

2. Sam is happy **about** / **of** starting college next week.

3. Tran is tired **about** / **of** working in a supermarket.

4. Louisa is thinking **about** / **in** going to school next semester.

5. I want to thank you **about** / **for** helping me.

4 Complete the sentences.

about finding a job	for driving me to work	of getting up early
about getting a scholarship	in learning about computers	of losing their jobs

1. I'm worried _about finding a job_____ .

2. Thank you _____ .

3. Serena is happy _____ .

4. Chang is tired _____ .

5. Lisa and Theo are afraid _____ .

6. Maurice is interested _____ .

5 Complete the sentences. Use the information in the chart.

Name	Feelings	Activity
Ron	excited	go to college
Miguel	afraid	lose his job
Vincent and Anna	happy	pay off their loan
Tim and Betsy	worried	get into debt
Steve	interested	buy a new car

1. Ron _is excited about going to college_____ .

2. Miguel _____ .

3. Vincent and Anna _____ .

4. Tim and Betsy _____ .

5. Steve _____ .

Check your answers. See page 139.

TRACK 24

1 Read and answer the questions. Then listen.

How many credit cards should you have?

How many credit cards do you have in your wallet? Are you worried about getting into debt? Many Americans carry four or five credit cards, but others have more than ten. Is it a good idea to have so many credit cards?

Some people almost never pay cash. It's easier to use a credit card. They use their credit cards for everything – food, clothes, gas, utility bills, and rent. However, when the bills arrive, people who have too many cards sometimes can't afford the minimum payments. It's also difficult to keep track of so many cards.

It's not uncommon to have store credit cards. Some stores offer a 10–15 percent discount when you use their credit card. They also offer coupons and other discounts. But be careful. The interest rates on these cards can be very high. It's a good idea to use a store credit card at your favorite store if you shop there often. But you should pay off the account balance immediately. That way, you won't pay any interest.

Debt counselors say that it's a good idea to have at least two cards. Use one card for everyday living expenses, and keep the other one for emergencies. They suggest choosing credit cards with low interest rates, keeping your account balance low, always trying to pay more than just the minimum payments, and having no more than six cards.

1. What happens to some people when they have too many credit cards?
   They can't afford the minimum payments.

2. What do some stores offer when you use their credit card?
   _____

3. Why is it important to pay off your account balance immediately?
   _____

4. How many credit cards do debt counselors say you should have?
   _____

Check your answers. See page 139.

2 Write four tips for using credit cards. Use the information from the article in Exercise 1.

1. *Choose credit cards with low interest rates.*

2. _____

3. _____

4. _____

3 Match.

1. minimum __e__   a. card
2. credit ____   b. budget
3. interest ____   c. counselor
4. debt ____   d. rate
5. family ____   e. payment

4 Complete the sentences. Use words in Exercise 3.

1. I don't have any _____credit_____ cards.

2. The _____ rate is very high.

3. We always make a family _____.

4. What is the _____ payment?

5. Why don't you talk to a debt _____?

5 Complete the sentences. Use words in Exercise 3.

1. I canceled my credit card because the ____interest rate____ was over 25 percent.

2. We made a _____. Now we can save enough every month.

3. When you use a _____, you borrow money and pay it back later.

4. We talked to a _____ to help us solve our financial problems.

5. The smallest payment you can make each month is the _____.

LESSON E Writing

1 Match the money problems with the suggestions.

1. I don't have enough money to buy lunch. __c__
2. I'm worried about being in debt. ____
3. I don't have enough nice clothes for work. ____
4. I'm too tired to cook dinner after work, but take-out meals are unhealthy. ____

a. Why don't you cook meals on the weekends and freeze them?
b. You could go to a thrift store.
c. How about bringing lunch from home?
d. You should see a debt counselor.

2 Read the letters. Answer the questions.

Dear Money Guy,

    I drive to work every day, but gas is very expensive. My car uses a lot of gas, and I can't afford to fill up my car. I also need to see an auto mechanic for repairs. I'm worried about having the car break down on the way to work. What should I do? Can you give me advice?

Worried Larry

Dear Worried Larry,

    I have a few suggestions for you. First, ask a co-worker to give you a ride to work, and you can share the cost of gas. Second, you could drive to work three times a week and take the bus twice a week. Finally, you could think about taking the bus for a couple of months and saving money for your car repairs. You might enjoy taking the bus. Then you could sell your car!

Money Guy

1. What are Worried Larry's problems?
   a. _Gas is very expensive._
   b. _____
   c. _____

2. What are Money Guy's suggestions?
   a. _____
   b. _____
   c. _____

Check your answers. See page 139.

3 Read the letter to Money Guy.

Dear Money Guy,

    I spend too much money on clothes. I don't really need new clothes, but when I go to the mall, I always want to buy something new. I use my store credit card. At first, I tried to pay off my bill every month. But now I have reached my spending limit, and the bills are too high. What should I do?

Clothes Crazy

4 Read the solutions. Write an answer to Clothes Crazy. Use *First*, *Second*, *Third*, and *Finally*.

Solution 1	Solution 2	Solution 3	Solution 4
Pay all your bills before you go back to the mall.	After you pay your bills, cancel your store credit card. Always pay cash.	Make a list of clothes you really need before you go shopping.	Go shopping with a friend. Ask your friend's advice before you buy anything.

Dear Clothes Crazy,

    I have a few suggestions for you. _____

_____

_____

_____

_____

_____

_____

_____

_____

_____

I hope this advice is helpful!

Money Guy

LESSON F Another view

1 Read the questions. Look at the credit card brochure. Then fill in the correct answers.

	City Spender credit card	Super Express credit card
Annual fee	• none	• 1st year free, then $75
Monthly interest rate	• 0% interest rate for the first six months • After six months, the interest rate is 13.4%	• 0% interest rate for the first three months • After three months, the interest rate is 11.49%
Rewards program	• Five points for every $1.00 spent	• One point for every $1.00 spent • 1,000 bonus points with your first purchase and 100 bonus points with your 100th purchase
Minimum monthly payment	• 1% of the account balance	• 2% of the account balance

1. What is the interest rate with a Super Express credit card after two months?
   ● 0%
   ⓑ 1%
   ⓒ 2%
   ⓓ 11.49%

2. What does the City Spender credit card offer?
   ⓐ bonus points with the first purchase
   ⓑ one reward point for every $5.00 spent
   ⓒ 0% interest for the first six months
   ⓓ 13.4% interest for the first three months

3. What does the Super Express credit card offer?
   ⓐ 0% interest for the first six months
   ⓑ one reward point for every dollar spent
   ⓒ no annual fee in the second year
   ⓓ none of the above

4. What is the minimum monthly payment with a City Spender credit card?
   ⓐ 0% of the account balance
   ⓑ 1% of the account balance
   ⓒ 2% of the account balance
   ⓓ 13.4% of the account balance

5. Which is true about both credit cards?
   ⓐ no annual fees in the first year
   ⓑ 2% minimum monthly payment
   ⓒ 0% interest for the first six months
   ⓓ all of the above

6. Which is true about both credit cards?
   ⓐ one point for every dollar spent
   ⓑ 11.49% interest for the first three months
   ⓒ both *a* and *b*
   ⓓ neither *a* nor *b*

Check your answers. See page 139.

2 Complete the sentences with a form of *get* or *take*.

1. Last year, we _____*took*_____ our vacation in August.

2. Becky can't understand her bank statement. She always _____ confused when she sees so many numbers.

3. My parents _____ very upset when they saw the balance on my credit card.

4. I like to study with Kenji because he _____ good notes.

5. I'm tired of shopping. Let's _____ a break and have a snack.

6. We should _____ a bus to go downtown. Taxis are too expensive.

7. Many people _____ nervous when they have to speak in front of a big group.

8. I think I'm _____ sick. I have a headache, and I'm really tired.

3 Write new sentences with a similar meaning. Use an expression from the box.

get dressed	got fired	take a trip
got divorced	take a nap	take notes

1. You should always <u>write down information</u> during class.
   You should always take notes during class.

2. Milos and Judy were married, but last month they <u>decided to stop being married</u>.
   _____

3. I'm tired. I'm going to <u>sleep for a short time</u>.
   _____

4. Harriet used to work for the phone company, but she <u>lost her job</u> last week.
   _____

5. It takes Lucy an hour to <u>put on her clothes</u>.
   _____

6. I'm going to <u>travel to another place</u> next month.
   _____

LESSON A Listening

1 Read and complete the paragraph. Then listen.

TRACK 25

| degree | employed | gets along | personnel | reliable | shift | strengths |

Marina is from Senegal and has been living in the United States for one year. She has been ___employed___ (1) as a cashier in a pharmacy for about six months. She has several _____ (2) as an employee. She is _____ (3) and friendly. She also _____ (4) well with her co-workers. She is taking business courses at night and wants to get a _____ (5) in hotel management.

Last week, she applied for a job as a reservations clerk at a big hotel. In the future, she hopes to get a job as an assistant manager or a manager. Today she got a call from the _____ (6) manager asking her to come in for an interview.

Marina is confident that she can do the job. She speaks English well, and she speaks French fluently. She knows how to use a computer, a copy machine, and a fax machine. But she can't work the night _____ (7) because of her business classes.

2 Complete the chart. Use the information about Marina in Exercise 1.

	Topic	Marina's answers
1.	job she is applying for	*reservations clerk*
2.	native country	
3.	current job	
4.	office machines she can use	
5.	strengths	

Check your answers. See page 139.

3 Answer the personnel manager's questions. Use the information about Marina in Exercise 1.

1. *A* Where are you from?

   B _I'm from Senegal._ _____

2. *A* What kind of work do you do?

   B _____

3. *A* What office machines can you use?

   B _____

4. *A* What other job skills do you have?

   B _____

5. *A* Are you taking any classes to improve your job skills?

   B _____

6. *A* What are your personal strengths?

   B _____

4 Complete the sentences.

background	employed	get along	interview	shift	strengths

1. I have many friends at school. I _____*get along*_____ with everybody.

2. I don't have a job now. I am not currently _____.

3. One of my _____ is that I am very reliable.

4. I have a job _____ next week.

5. I can't work during the day. I need to work the night _____.

6. Can you tell me more about your _____? I'd like to know more about you.

5 Listen. Then circle the correct words.

TRACK 26

1. Geraldo is applying for a job as **a building manager / an electrician**.

2. Geraldo is from **Argentina / Canada**.

3. At the moment he's working part-time as a **plumber / custodian**.

4. Geraldo tells Ms. Lee that he is **hard-working / qualified**.

LESSON B Present perfect continuous

Study the chart and explanation on page 129.

1 Complete the chart.

a long time	morning	September	Tuesday	2005	week
day	one hour	three months	2:00 p.m.	two weeks	year

for	since	all
a long time		

2 Write sentences. Use the present perfect continuous with *for*, *since*, and *all*.

1. Kendra / work / in the library / October

   Kendra has been working in the library since October.

2. Frank and Marta / study computers / two years

   _____

3. Carla / look for a job / January

   _____

4. I / wait for an interview / 1:30 p.m.

   _____

5. You / talk on the phone / two hours

   _____

6. We / use the library computers / morning

   _____

7. Kemal / drive a cab / 20 years

   _____

8. Gloria / cook / day

   _____

Check your answers. See page 139.

3 Write questions and two answers. Use the present perfect continuous with *for* and *since*.

1. Alicia and Claire started painting the house at 11:00 a.m. It is now 11:30 a.m.

   A How long *have Alicia and Claire been painting the house* _____?

   B Since *11:00 a.m.* _____

   For *30 minutes.* _____

2. Inez started cooking at 4:00 p.m. It is now 6:00 p.m.

   A How long _____?

   B Since _____

   For _____

3. Tony and Leon started studying computers on June 1st. Today is July 1st.

   A How long _____?

   B Since _____

   For _____

4. Yoshi started working in the hotel on Tuesday – five days ago.

   A How long _____?

   B Since _____

   For _____

5. I started using a computer in August. It is now November.

   A How long _____?

   B Since _____

   For _____

6. Lenka started driving this morning at 10:00 a.m. It is now 1:00 p.m.

   A How long _____?

   B Since _____

   For _____

7. Juan started attending this school three weeks ago. It is now February 5th.

   A How long _____?

   B Since _____

   For _____

LESSON C Phrasal verbs

Study the explanation and list of phrasal verbs on page 132.

1 Complete the sentences.

away	back	down	out	up

1. I'm busy now. Could you please call _____*back*_____ later?

2. Could you please fill _____ this application?

3. I don't want to listen to music. Could you turn _____ the volume?

4. Could you clean _____ your room, please?

5. Please put _____ your dictionary. You can't use a dictionary during the test.

2 Look at the words in bold. Write the sentences again with *him*, *it*, or *them*.

1. Anton needs to turn down **the music**.

   He *needs to turn it down* _____.

2. Rita is cleaning up **the kitchen**.

   She _____.

3. Martine is throwing away **old newspapers**.

   She _____.

4. The students are putting away **their books**.

   They _____.

5. I need to call back **my father**.

   I _____.

3 Complete the sentences. Use phrasal verbs and *him*, *it*, or *them*.

1. These clothes are clean. Please put _____*them away*_____.

2. Your room is a mess! Please clean _____.

3. Your husband just called and left a message. Please call _____.

4. The volume on your cell phone is not loud enough. Please turn _____.

5. Here is the job application. Please fill _____.

Check your answers. See page 140.

4 Add the missing word in each sentence.

1. I don't have time to call back. (him)
   him (inserted above "call back")

2. There's too much trash. Please throw out. (it)

3. We don't need these winter jackets anymore. Please put them. (away)

4. I want to watch TV. Let's turn on. (it)

5 Complete the sentences.

call back	clean up	hand out	put away

1.

She's _____*putting away*_____ her clothes.

She's __*putting*__ her clothes __*away*__.

She's __*putting*__ them __*away*__.

2.

He's _____ the tests.

He's _____ the tests _____.

He's _____ them _____.

3.

She's _____ her kitchen.

She's _____ her kitchen _____.

She's _____ it _____.

4.

He's _____ Doctor Kim.

He's _____ Doctor Kim _____.

He's _____ him _____.

LESSON D Reading

1 **Scan the blog. Answer the questions. Then listen and read.**

TRACK 27

1. Who wrote the blog?

   Ivan wrote the blog.

2. What is the blog about?

   _____

3. How long has the writer been writing the blog?

   _____

4. What does the writer ask readers to do?

   _____

⚫ ⚪ ⚪

Ivan's Blog

Friday 3/06	It's been a busy week! I've been learning a lot and I'm excited about learning more.
Thursday 3/05	Today I was really tired. I almost fell asleep on the train coming home. I was too tired to cook dinner and fell asleep in front of the TV. This job is harder than I expected. I feel a bit depressed.
Wednesday 3/04	Today I went to lunch with two of my co-workers. I think I'm starting to make friends here! They told me it's hard work – I'm worried about that, but I'm not going to give up!
Tuesday 3/03	I've been trying very hard to talk to everyone here because it's important to network. I'm not very confident yet, but I have been smiling at everyone and introducing myself. Most people are really friendly. But some are too serious, and they don't say much!
Monday 3/02	The first day in my new job! All morning, I filled out forms for the human resources department. In the afternoon, I met the other people on my team and learned how to use the copier. There's a lot to learn, but I'll try to be patient.

If you have any tips about starting a new job – please share them with me!

Check your answers. See page 140.

2 Number the events from Ivan's blog in Exercise 1 in the order they happened.

____ Ivan almost fell asleep on the train home.

____ Ivan met the other people on his team.

____ Ivan had lunch with his co-workers.

_1_ Ivan filled out human resources forms.

____ Ivan was too tired to cook dinner.

____ Ivan learned how to use the copier.

3 Match the days with Ivan's feelings. Use the information in Ivan's blog in Exercise 1.

1. Monday _d_

2. Tuesday ____

3. Wednesday ____

4. Thursday ____

5. Friday ____

a. not confident

b. depressed

c. excited

d. trying to be patient

e. a little worried

4 Find the adjectives in Ivan's blog. Underline them. Then circle the definition that best fits the reading.

1. confident   (a.) sure of yourself   b. firm

2. serious   a. critical   b. quiet

3. depressed   a. unhappy   b. sick

4. busy   a. filled with people   b. working hard

5. excited   a. nervous   b. happy

6. patient   a. not angry   b. able to wait

5 Complete the chart. Use a dictionary to help you.

	Adjective	Noun
1.	confident	_confidence_
2.	excited	
3.	serious	
4.	patient	
5.	depressed	

LESSON E Writing

1 Complete the thank-you letter. Use the information in the chart.

Your name	Sarah Bonarelli
Your address	264 West Street, Minneapolis, MN 55404
Today's date	August 15, 2013
Name of interviewer	Ms. Ann Robinson
Interviewer's title	Office Manager
Address of interviewer	City Office Services, 2321 Central Avenue, Minneapolis, MN 55409
Date of interview	August 14, 2013
Reason for saying thank you	Job interview on Friday, August 14th
Something specific you appreciate	You saw the office and learned about the company.

264 West Street _____

_____

_____

_____

_____

_____

_____

_____

Dear _____ :

   I would like to thank you for the _____ I had with you on _____ . I appreciate the time you spent with me.

I enjoyed seeing the _____ and learning more about the _____ .

   Thank you again for your time. I hope to hear from you soon.

Sincerely,

_____

Check your answers. See page 140.

2 Tony Wilson went on a job interview. Write Tony's thank-you letter. Use the information from his notes.

Notes
- Interview with Mr. Alan Barlow, Personnel Manager
- December 18, 2013, 10:00 a.m.
- Superstar Electric Company
  465 Main Avenue, Houston, TX 77028
- He told me about the training program.
- He gave me the employee handbook to read.
  It helped me learn more about the company.

13 New Street
Houston, TX 77297
December 18, 2013

_____
_____
_____
_____
_____

_____ :

_____

_____

_____

_____

_____

_____

                                    _____ ,

                                    _____

LESSON F Another view

1 **Read the questions. Look at the chart. Then fill in the correct answers.**

Changing Job Market 2010 to 2020				
Occupation	Jobs in 2010	Jobs in 2020	Change	Percent Change
Home health aides	1,017,700	1,723,900	+706,200	+69.4%
Registered nurses	2,737,400	3,449,300	+711,900	+26.0%
Truck drivers	1,604,800	1,934,900	+330,100	+20.6%
Post office mail carriers	316,700	278,600	-38,100	-12.0%
Construction workers	998,800	1,211,200	+212,400	+21.3%
Fast food cooks	530,500	511,400	-19,100	-3.6%
Source: U.S. Bureau of Labor Statistics				

1. Which job will increase the most in 10 years?
   Ⓐ registered nurse
   ● home health aide
   Ⓒ post office mail carrier
   Ⓓ truck driver

2. Which is probably *not* a good job to plan for in 2020?
   Ⓐ truck driver
   Ⓑ fast food cook
   Ⓒ home health aide
   Ⓓ construction worker

3. According to the chart, which is probably the best job area in 2020?
   Ⓐ fast food restaurants
   Ⓑ transportation
   Ⓒ construction
   Ⓓ health care

4. Which job employed the most people in 2010?
   Ⓐ home health aide
   Ⓑ truck driver
   Ⓒ construction worker
   Ⓓ registered nurse

5. How many construction jobs were there in 2010?
   Ⓐ 1,211,200
   Ⓑ 212,400
   Ⓒ 998,800
   Ⓓ 530,500

6. For which jobs do the numbers go down and not up?
   Ⓐ post office mail carriers and fast food cooks
   Ⓑ truck drivers and mail carriers
   Ⓒ registered nurses and home health aides
   Ⓓ construction workers and fast food cooks

Check your answers. See page 140.

2 Complete the sentences. Use the present continuous and the present perfect continuous.

1. Eliza / read a mystery story

   Eliza's reading a mystery story now.

   _She's been reading_____ it for

   the last three hours.

2. The Jensens / live in Miami

   _____ now.

   _____ there

   for three years.

3. I / study Russian

   _____ in the

   language lab now.

   _____ since

   last year.

4. Esteban / look for a job

   _____ now.

   _____ for six

   months.

5. Jun / organize his papers

   _____ now.

   _____ them

   since this morning.

6. Julie / write her blog

   _____ at

   home now.

   _____ since

   last January.

3 Complete the story. Use the present continuous or the present perfect continuous.

Megan ___has been working___ as an office assistant in a big
          1. work
computer company for about five years. Lately, she

_____ bored with her job. It's the same routine
       2. feel
every day. Recently, she _____ for some different
                              3. look
career ideas. Last week, she saw an article about a job in a safari

park in Botswana, a country in Africa. So now she _____ to apply
                                                          4. plan
for a job there. At the moment, she _____ a letter to the safari
                                          5. write
park, and she _____ a lot of books about Botswana. She says, "For
                   6. read
the last five years, I _____ to work at the same place every day. Now
                            7. go
I _____ the first step toward an exciting change in my life."
      8. make

LESSON **A** Listening

1 **Complete the conversation. Then listen.**

TRACK 28

| broke into | crime | robbed | robber | stole |

ANTON Did you hear that someone ___*broke into*___ Arthur's car last night and

_____ his computer?

             2

FRED That's terrible!

ANTON Arthur's really upset. He uses that computer for work, and it has the names and

addresses of his customers in it.

FRED What's he going to do?

ANTON Well, the computer has a secret code in it. If the _____ tries to use

                                                3

it, an alarm will go off and tell the police where it is.

FRED That's smart! By the way, did you hear that someone _____ the

                                           4

bank on South Street last week?

ANTON There is so much _____ in this neighborhood now!

                                5

2 **Circle the correct answers. Use the information in Exercise 1.**

1. What happened to Arthur?
   a. Someone stole his car.
   b. Someone stole his computer.
   c. Someone broke into his house.
   d. Someone broke his computer.

2. Why is Arthur upset?
   a. His car is broken.
   b. His car is expensive.
   c. His computer has a special alarm.
   d. His computer has important
      information on it.

3. What will happen if the robber uses
   the computer?
   a. The police will find the car.
   b. The police will find the computer.
   c. The police will call Arthur.
   d. The police will call the robber.

4. What happened at the bank?
   a. Someone left the bank.
   b. Someone closed the bank.
   c. Someone cleaned up the bank.
   d. Someone stole cash from the bank.

Check your answers. See page 140.

3 Complete the story.

break into	came over	got into	robber	stole

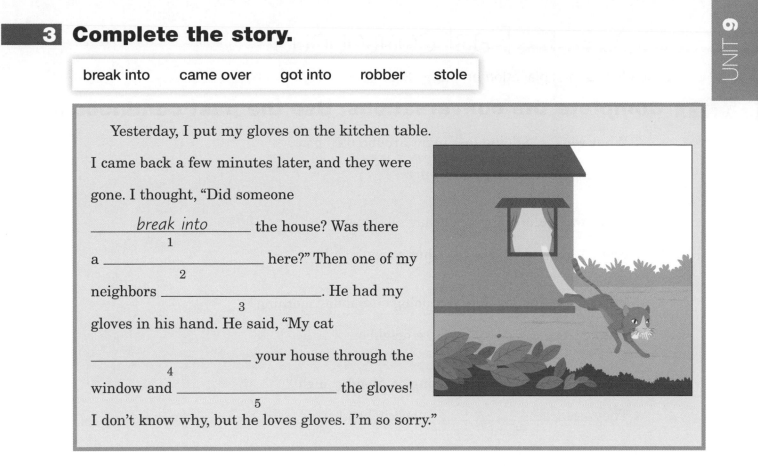

Yesterday, I put my gloves on the kitchen table.
I came back a few minutes later, and they were
gone. I thought, "Did someone

_____*break into*_____ the house? Was there
                1

a _____ here?" Then one of my
            2

neighbors _____. He had my
                  3

gloves in his hand. He said, "My cat

_____ your house through the
            4

window and _____ the gloves!
                  5

I don't know why, but he loves gloves. I'm so sorry."

4 Circle the correct words.

1. Two men **robbed / stole** a bank on Main Street.

2. The same night, three robbers **broke into / came over** a supermarket on Park Avenue.

3. The men made a big **crime / mess** in the store. Cans and bottles were all over the floor.

4. The robbers set off the alarm, so the police **came over / got into** right away.

5. The police said, "We were busy with two **crimes / robbers** on the same night."

5 What happened in the story? Listen. Then check (✓) the correct answer.

TRACK 29

☐ The police caught the robbers when they were driving down Lombard Avenue.

☐ The robbers ran away because the car didn't have any gas in it.

☐ The robbers parked the car because the police were chasing them.

LESSON B Past continuous

Study the chart and explanation on page 130.

1 Complete the conversations. Use the past continuous.

1. **A** What were you doing last night around 6:00 p.m.?

   B I _____ *was eating* _____ dinner.
   (eat)

2. **A** What was Julie doing yesterday afternoon?

   B She _____ her cousin's children.
   (babysit)

3. **A** What were Phuong and Tim doing on Sunday morning?

   B They _____ a neighbor.
   (visit)

4. **A** What were Lisa and Alan doing on Monday night?

   B They _____ the kitchen.
   (clean)

5. **A** What was Kemal doing at 4:30 p.m.?

   B He was _____ a newspaper.
   (read)

2 What were these people doing at 8:00 a.m. yesterday? Complete the sentences.

| drive | knit | sleep | study | talk | watch |

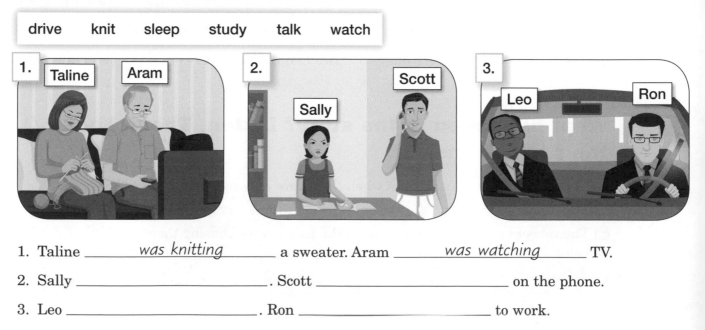

1. Taline _____ *was knitting* _____ a sweater. Aram _____ *was watching* _____ TV.

2. Sally _____ . Scott _____ on the phone.

3. Leo _____ . Ron _____ to work.

Check your answers. See page 140.

3 Look at the chart. Answer the questions.

	9:00 a.m.	2:00 p.m.	5:00 p.m.
Anna	eat breakfast	study English	clean the house
Pete	paint the bedroom	study English	watch a movie
Louise	drive to work	attend a meeting	clean the house
Fareed	drive to work	read a book	watch a movie

1. **A** Was Louise studying English at 2:00 p.m.?

   B _No, she wasn't._

2. **A** Were Anna and Louise cleaning the house at 5:00 p.m.?

   B _____

3. **A** Were Louise and Fareed driving to work at 9:00 a.m.?

   B _____

4. **A** Was Pete studying English at 5:00 p.m.?

   B _____

4 Write questions and answers. Use the present continuous and the chart in Exercise 3.

1. Anna / 9:00 a.m.

   A What _was Anna doing at 9:00 a.m._____?

   B _She was eating breakfast._____

2. Fareed / 2:00 p.m.

   A What _____?

   B _____

3. Pete / 9:00 a.m.

   A What _____?

   B _____

4. Anna and Pete / 2:00 p.m.

   A What _____?

   B _____

Check your answers. See page 140.

LESSON C Past continuous and simple past

Study the explanation on page 133.

1 Underline the past continuous in each sentence.

1. We <u>were jogging</u> in the park when it started to rain.
2. I ran out of gas while I was driving to work.
3. Seema was having lunch with a friend when someone stole her car.
4. When the fire started, I was making cookies in the kitchen.
5. While the neighbors were attending a meeting, someone called the police.
6. Fatima was talking on the phone when her husband came home.

2 Complete the paragraph. Use the past continuous or the simple past.

    While I _____*was working*_____ in the garden yesterday,
                        1. work

I _____*heard*_____ a loud noise in the street. It sounded
       2. hear

like a car accident. When I looked in the street, two strangers

_____. One of them looked very upset.
      3. talk

The other driver _____ too fast when she
                        4. drive

_____ a tree. The tree then _____
      5. hit   6. fall

on the other person's car. What a mess!

Check your answers. See page 140.

3 Write sentences. Use the past continuous and the simple past.

1. While we (eat lunch), the lights (go out).

   While we were eating lunch, the lights went out.

2. Ellen (sleep) when the fire alarm (go off) in her home.

   _____

3. When we (get) a parking ticket, we (shop) at the mall.

   _____

4. While Francisco (jog), it (start) to rain.

   _____

5. While I (cook) dinner, my husband (attend) a meeting.

   _____

6. Julio and Tia (work) in the garden when Julio (fall) off the ladder.

   _____

4 Combine the sentences. Use the past continuous and the simple past.

1. Chang watched TV. The fire alarm went off.

   While *Chang was watching TV, the fire alarm went off* _____ .

2. The lights went out. We visited our neighbors.

   When _____ , _____ .

3. I baked a cake. An earthquake started.

   _____ when _____ .

4. We ate dinner. A thief stole my purse.

   _____ when _____ .

5. It began to rain. Fernando and Luis painted the house.

   _____ while _____ .

6. We drove in a bad storm. A tree fell on our car.

   _____ when _____ .

7. Maria took a grammar test. Yan did her homework.

   While _____ , _____ .

Check your answers. See page 140.

1 Read and circle the correct answers. Then listen.

TRACK 30

A Helping Hand

by Rodrigo and Elena Gonzalez

A year ago, a huge hurricane hit our state. It was the largest hurricane in 40 years, and it destroyed many of the homes in our neighborhood. Everyone had to evacuate. Some people lost everything – their home, their furniture, their car. Luckily, our home was OK, but we felt we had to help our neighbors.

The next day, we started to collect money, clothes, shoes, and food. Everyone was very generous and gave as much as they could. We used the money to buy food and water bottles. Two days later, we had three cars full of supplies. We took them over to the park and set up a shelter.

For the next three days, we stayed at the shelter. While people were looking for their families and gathering their things, we cooked food, served tea and coffee, and handed out clothes, food, and water. They were really glad to have our support. And we were very glad to have the chance to help them. One year later, we started a neighborhood organization to help everyone in our community in difficult times. It's important to know you can get help from your neighbors.

1. What is the main idea of this article?
   a. Hurricanes are dangerous.
   b. People should ask for help.
   c. Some people lost everything.
   d. Neighbors should help each other.

2. Which event happened first?
   a. The writers set up a shelter.
   b. The writers bought food and water.
   c. The writers collected food and money.
   d. The writers started a neighborhood organization.

3. What happened when the writers started to collect supplies?
   a. People didn't give any money.
   b. People gave clothes, food, and money.
   c. People gave tents and water bottles.
   d. People did not give very much.

4. Why did the writers feel good?
   a. They had to evacuate.
   b. They got to rebuild their home.
   c. They didn't need help.
   d. They were able to help their neighbors.

Check your answers. See page 141.

2 Underline the time phrases. Answer the questions.

1. We moved to this country <u>in 2010.</u> <u>A year later</u> we had a baby.

   A When did they have a baby?

   B *In 2011.*_____

2. A hurricane destroyed our home in August. Two months later, we rebuilt our home.

   A When did they rebuild their home?

   B _____

3. In July, there was a terrible fire in our town. For the next three months, we collected money and clothes.

   A When did they stop collecting money and clothes?

   B _____

4. At 6:00 p.m., we heard the fire alarm. Four minutes later, we evacuated the building.

   A At what time did they evacuate the building?

   B _____

3 Match the bold words with the correct meaning.

1. a. They were **gathering** apples in the backyard.
   b. A crowd was **gathering** in the street.
   _b_ meeting   _a_ collecting

2. a. Daniel needs a scholarship to **support** his college education.
   b. Thank you for your **support** after the hurricane.
   ____ help   ____ pay for

3. a. A thief **grabbed** my wallet on the bus.
   b. I **grabbed** as many photographs as I could during the fire.
   ____ stole   ____ took quickly

4. a. They gave us a **generous** amount of money.
   b. Our neighbors were very **generous** to us after the earthquake.
   ____ large   ____ helpful

5. a. We **lost** everything in the earthquake.
   b. We **lost** the game.
   ____ didn't win   ____ don't have it anymore

LESSON E Writing

1 Read the story. Then answer the questions.

One evening last week, I was driving home from work. I was driving slowly through my neighborhood when my cell phone rang. I pulled over to the curb and answered it. It was my wife. She asked me to pick up some food for dinner from the supermarket on the way home. I was turning off my cell phone and pulling back out when a cat ran across the street. I immediately turned the car to the right, and I hit a fire hydrant. Water went everywhere.

Luckily, I was OK. I didn't hit the cat, but the car was damaged. Firefighters came to fix the fire hydrant. The police arrived, and I had to fill out an accident report. While I was talking to the police, my wife called again. She wanted to know what happened to me. I said, "Well, I think I'll be a little late tonight."

1. What is the story about?

   The story is about a car accident.

2. When did the accident happen?

3. Where did the accident happen?

4. What was the writer doing when the story started?

5. Why did the accident happen?

6. How did the story end?

Check your answers. See page 141.

2 Look at the pictures. Circle the correct answers.

Joe

1. When did the story start?   a. at 5:55 a.m.   (b.) at 5:55 p.m.

2. Where did the story happen?   a. on a train   b. on a plane

3. What was Joe doing when the
   story started?   a. reading   b. talking

4. What was next to Joe?   a. a friend   b. a box

5. What happened while he was
   getting off the train?   a. He found his box.   b. He saw a friend.

6. What happened when the
   train doors closed?   a. He remembered his box.   b. He forgot his book.

7. How did the story end?   a. The doors opened,   b. The doors closed,
                                       and he took his box.   and he lost his box.

3 Write a paragraph about what happened to Joe in Exercise 2. Use the past continuous. Write at least one sentence with *when* and one sentence with *while*.

One evening at 5:55 p.m., Joe was sitting on a train.

_____

_____

_____

_____

_____

_____

_____

_____

_____

Check your answers. See page 141.

LESSON F Another view

Read the questions. Look at the chart. Then fill in the correct answers.

Top ten cities in the U.S. in rank order by population size	2000	2010
New York, NY	1	1
Los Angeles, CA	2	2
Chicago, IL	3	3
Houston, TX	4	4
Philadelphia, PA	5	5
Phoenix, AZ	6	6
San Antonio, TX	9	7
San Diego, CA	7	8
Dallas, TX	8	9
San José, CA	11	10

Sources: U.S. Census Bureau. www.census.gov/prod/cen2010/briefs/c2010br-01.pdf

1. Which state has the highest number of top ten cities by population size?
   - ● Texas
   - Ⓑ Arizona
   - Ⓒ California
   - Ⓓ New York

2. Which of the following cities had the same ranking in 2000 and in 2010?
   - Ⓐ Dallas
   - Ⓑ San José
   - Ⓒ San Antonio
   - Ⓓ Los Angeles

3. Which of the following cities had a different ranking?
   - Ⓐ New York
   - Ⓑ Houston
   - Ⓒ San Diego
   - Ⓓ Philadelphia

4. Which city's rank order changed the most?
   - Ⓐ Chicago
   - Ⓑ Dallas
   - Ⓒ Phoenix
   - Ⓓ San Antonio

5. Which city was not on the top ten list in 2000?
   - Ⓐ Dallas
   - Ⓑ San José
   - Ⓒ San Diego
   - Ⓓ Phoenix

6. Which city had a smaller population in 2010 than it did in 2000?
   - Ⓐ Chicago
   - Ⓑ Dallas
   - Ⓒ San Antonio
   - Ⓓ Philadelphia

Check your answers. See page 141.

2 How do these sentences use the present continuous? Mark them N (now), OE (ongoing event), or NF (near future).

_N_ 1. It's snowing outside.

____ 2. My husband is cleaning the snow off the sidewalk.

____ 3. Later today, we're going shopping.

____ 4. We're cooking dinner for some friends tonight.

____ 5. We're both taking cooking classes at the Culinary Institute this month.

____ 6. Next week, we're learning to prepare some Asian foods.

____ 7. I'm volunteering to cook at the community center this year.

____ 8. At the moment, I'm just watching the snow come down.

3 Look at the chart. Complete the sentences.

	Greg	Nicole	Hamoud
Now	work in garden	fill out a job application	call some friends to ask them to give food
Ongoing event	take a class at the garden center	try to find a job as a salesperson	collect food for a family that lost their home in a flood
Near future	take some vegetables to the county fair	go to a department store for an interview	take the food to the family

Greg:

1. This summer, _Greg is taking a class at the garden center_ .

2. Next Saturday, he _____.

3. At the moment, _____.

Nicole:

4. This month, _____.

5. Right now, _____.

6. On Friday, _____.

Hamoud:

7. This week, _____.

8. Next Saturday, _____.

9. At the moment, _____.

LESSON A Listening

1 Read and complete the paragraph. Then listen.

TRACK 31

| books | days off | discounts | reserve | round-trip | tax |

Fabiola has three _____days off_____ next week. She wants to go on vacation.
$\overset{}{\underset{1}{}}$

She went on the Internet and found some good _____ on flights
$\overset{}{\underset{2}{}}$

to Washington, D.C. She can get a _____ ticket for $95.00 if she
$\overset{}{\underset{3}{}}$

_____ her flight five days ahead. The flight takes one hour. It leaves
$\overset{}{\underset{4}{}}$

at 2:00 p.m. on Monday, and the return flight leaves Washington, D.C., at 11:00 a.m.

on Wednesday. The hotel costs $120 a night plus _____, which is
$\overset{}{\underset{5}{}}$

$14.50 per night.

If she takes the train, the trip will take three hours. The train leaves at

8:00 a.m. on Monday, and the return train leaves Washington, D.C., at 6:00 p.m.

on Tuesday. She does not need to _____ a hotel room for two nights.
$\overset{}{\underset{6}{}}$

The train costs $175.00, but she can stay just one night and still have two full days

of sightseeing.

2 Complete the chart. Use the information in Exercise 1.

	Cost of transportation	Cost of lodging	Total cost
By plane	$95.00		
By train			

Fabiola's trip is cheaper if she travels by _____.

Check your answers. See page 141.

3 Make sentences. Match the sentence parts.

1. You should reserve a room early __d__   a. come here during the summer.
2. You should book a flight in advance ____   b. doesn't usually include tax.
3. The advertised room rate ____   c. to get the best discounts.
4. Many tourists ____   d. because hotels are very busy at this time.

4 Look at the bold words. Write sentences. Use words from the box with a similar meaning.

days off	discount	high	reserve

1. Room rates are **expensive** in the summer. _Room rates are high in the summer._
2. You can get a **cheaper rate** if you book ahead. _____
3. You can **book** your hotel room online. _____
4. Sam has three **vacation days**. _____

5 Solve the problems.

1. Sal and his wife Dana need a vacation. They want to take a weekend trip to Miami and stay two nights. They have never been there before. They can get a round-trip plane ticket for $150.00 each. The hotel costs $150.00 per night plus tax. The tax is $19.00 dollars per night. How much will their transportation and lodging cost? _____

2. Joanna and her husband Andy have a few days off, and they want to take a vacation. They have $1,200.00 to spend. They want to go to Orlando for three nights. Round-trip plane tickets cost $250.00 for each person. The hotel costs $120.00 plus $13.00 for tax each night. How much money will they have after they have paid for transportation and lodging? _____

6 Listen. Then mark the sentences as S (Sure) or NS (Not Sure).

TRACK 32

__NS__ 1. Arturo and Hana will stay at the Mount Green Ski Lodge.

____ 2. Arturo and Hana will go skiing at Mount Green this weekend.

____ 3. Arturo and Hana will borrow a cabin from Arturo's friend Mark.

____ 4. Arturo's office will be closed on Friday.

LESSON B Conditionals

Study the explanation on page 133.

1 Circle the correct forms of the verbs.

1. If we (get) / **will get** a few days off, we **go** / (will go) to the beach.

2. Rosa **travels** / **will travel** by plane if the tickets **aren't** / **won't be** too expensive.

3. If the weather **is** / **will be** good, we **ride** / **will ride** our bicycles.

4. If Charlie **visits** / **will visit** San Diego, he **stays** / **will stay** with his sister.

5. If we **don't** / **won't** find a cheap hotel, we **don't** / **won't** go to New York.

2 Look at the pictures. Answer the questions.

1.

2.

3.

4.

1. What will Jack do if his friends come over this afternoon?

   If Jack's friends come over this afternoon, they'll play soccer.

2. What will the Perez family do if the weather is good?

   _____

3. What will Stacey do if she has the day off?

   _____

4. What will Robert do this weekend if it rains?

   _____

Check your answers. See page 141.

3 **Complete the conversation. Use the simple present or future form of the verbs.**

A What will you do this summer if you have a few days off?

B If I ___*have*___ enough money, I _____ my family in California.
        1. have   2. visit

A That sounds fun! What _____ you _____ if you _____
                        3. do   4. not / have

enough money?

B I guess I'll stay home. What about you?

A If my brother _____ from Chicago, we _____ camping. But if he
            5. come   6. go

_____ , I _____ my friends in Houston.
  7. not / come   8. visit

4 **Write questions with *if*. Then answer the questions.**

1. Brian / do / have time off this summer

   A What *will Brian do if he has time off this summer* ?
   B He *will go swimming* .
                    (go swimming)

2. Tam and Chen / do / the weather is beautiful this weekend

   A What _____?
   B They _____.
              (work in the garden)

3. Sara / do / get some extra money for her birthday

   A What _____?
   B She _____.
             (go shopping)

4. you / do / have a three-day weekend

   A What _____?
   B I _____.
             (go hiking)

5. we / do / the weather is bad

   A What _____?
   B We _____.
            (clean the house)

Check your answers. See page 141.

LESSON C Future time clauses

Study the explanation on page 133.

TRACK 33

1 **Read and complete the sentences. Use the correct form of the verb. Then listen.**

Sanjit is planning a trip to Colorado. He has
decided to make a list of things he needs to do
before he ___*leaves*___ . Before he _____
              1. leave   2. go
on his trip, he _____ some books about
                3. read
Colorado. After he _____ the books, he
                   4. read
_____ a map and choose the best route for
     5. find
his trip. He _____ some campsites and make
          6. choose
reservations before he _____. On the day before he _____,
                   7. leave   8. leave
he _____ some food and first-aid supplies. He _____ some gas at
   9. buy   10. get
the gas station, too. After he does all that, he _____ his baggage into the car.
                                                           11. put
Then he'll be ready for his trip!

2 **Complete the sentences. Use the simple present or future with *will*.**

1. Victor / book a flight to Dallas / talk to a travel agent

    Before *Victor books a flight to Dallas* , *he will talk to a travel agent* .

2. Victor / make a hotel reservation / fly to Dallas

    _____ before _____ .

3. Victor / clean up the house / leave for the airport

    After _____ , _____ .

4. Victor / go through security / check in

    _____ after _____ .

5. Victor / get on the plane / turn off his cell phone

    Before _____ , _____ .

Check your answers. See page 141.

3 Look at Pedro's calendar. Write sentences about his plans. Use *before* and *after*.

Monday, November 26		Tuesday, November 27	
9:30–5:30 p.m.	Work	9:30–5:30 p.m.	Work
6:00 p.m.	Buy concert tickets	6:15 p.m.	Meet Nick
7:00 p.m.	Invite Nick to the concert	6:30 p.m.	Eat dinner at a restaurant
7:30 p.m.	Make dinner reservations	8:30 p.m.	Concert

1. Pedro / buy the concert tickets / invite Nick to the concert

   a. *Pedro will buy concert tickets before he invites Nick to the concert.*

   b. *Pedro will invite Nick to the concert after he buys concert tickets.*

2. He / invite Nick to the concert / make dinner reservations

   a. *He will invite Nick to the concert before* _____

   b. *He will make dinner reservations after* _____

3. He / meet Nick / finish work

   a. _____

   b. _____

4. He / go to the concert / eat dinner at a restaurant

   a. _____

   b. _____

4 Complete the conversations.

1. **A** What *will you do before you go on your trip* _____? (before)

   B Before I go on my trip, I will learn a few words in French.

2. **A** What _____? (before)

   B Before Trina goes on vacation, she will get a passport.

3. **A** Where _____? (after)

   B They will go to Philadelphia after they leave New York.

4. **A** What _____? (before)

   B Suzanna will buy a cup of coffee before she reads the newspaper.

Check your answers. See page 141.

LESSON **D** Reading

TRACK 34

The Statue of Liberty

The Statue of Liberty is one of the most popular tourist sights in New York City and a symbol of freedom for many Americans. The statue is on Liberty Island in the middle of New York Harbor. The people of France gave the statue to the people of the United States in 1886 as a gift of friendship.

Many people call the statue by its popular name, "Lady Liberty." The statue is a woman wearing a long robe and a crown with seven points. The points represent the seven continents and seven seas. She holds a flat piece of stone in her left hand and a burning torch high in her right hand. The stone has the date "JULY IV MDCCLXXVI" (July 4, 1776), the day of America's independence from Britain. There are 354 steps inside the statue and 25 windows in the crown. The 25 windows represent the 25 natural minerals of the earth.

It takes a lot of work to keep the Statue of Liberty in good condition. Sometimes the statue is closed for repairs. At these times, visitors are still able to visit the island and tour the park, but they aren't allowed to go into the statue. When the Statue of Liberty is open, visitors can learn about the statue at the museum in the base of the statue. A limited number of people can get a pass and climb up into the crown. From there, they can see a wonderful view of New York Harbor and the city's skyline.

To get to the Statue of Liberty, you must board a ferry. Private boats are not allowed to land on the island. It's a good idea to buy your tickets in advance, as the lines can be very long, and sometimes the tickets sell out.

1. The article gives information about the history of the statue.   (T)   F
2. The article describes the statue.   T   F
3. The article gives information about how to visit the statue.   T   F
4. The statue is over 300 years old.   T   F
5. The torch is in Lady Liberty's left hand.   T   F
6. France gave the statue as a gift in 1776.   T   F
7. Lady Liberty's crown has seven points.   T   F
8. You cannot buy tickets in advance to see the Statue of Liberty.   T   F

Check your answers. See page 141.

2 Answer the questions. Use the information in Exercise 1.

1. What is the main topic of the article?

   The Statue of Liberty is the main topic of this article.

2. Where is the statue located?

   _____

3. What happened in 1886?

   _____

4. Why did the people of France give the statue to the United States?

   _____

5. Why does July 4, 1776, appear on the statue?

   _____

6. How many steps are inside the statue?

   _____

7. What can you see from inside the crown?

   _____

8. How do you get to the Statue of Liberty?

   _____

3 Scan the article for the bold words. Underline them. Then circle the words with a similar meaning.

1. **sights**
   a. attractions
   b. parks

2. **symbol**
   a. sign
   b. gift

3. **gift**
   a. promise
   b. present

4. **robe**
   a. dress
   b. jacket

5. **torch**
   a. pen
   b. fire

6. **independence**
   a. freedom
   b. friendship

7. **pass**
   a. entrance
   b. ticket

8. **board**
   a. get on
   b. get off

1 **Read the paragraph. Then answer the questions.**

Central Park

Central Park, one of the most popular tourist attractions in New York City, is popular because it offers something for everyone. It is right in the heart of the city and is a perfect place to relax after a shopping trip or before you go to the theater. The zoo is open every day. If your children like animals, they will love the children's zoo, where children can touch animals such as goats and sheep. Older children can go to a beginner climbing course with special indoor and outdoor climbing walls. If the weather is nice, you can enjoy the beautiful weather and row boats on the lake. If you love culture and music, you'll enjoy one of the concerts or a theater performance of Shakespeare in the open-air theater. Finally, if you feel tired after a day of sightseeing and shopping, you can take a relaxing and romantic ride around the park in a horse-drawn carriage.

1. What is the main idea of the paragraph?

    Central Park is a popular attraction because it offers something for everyone.

2. What are four examples of things to do in Central Park?

    a. _____

    b. _____

    c. _____

    d. _____

3. What is the conclusion?

    _____

Check your answers. See page 141.

2 Read the information. Then write a paragraph about Hollywood. Include a main idea, at least three examples of things to do in Hollywood, and a conclusion.

VISIT HOLLYWOOD
Birthplace of the Movies! Los Angeles, California

Visit movie studios

Walk along the Hollywood Walk of Fame

See the footprints of movie stars

Go to a concert at the Hollywood Bowl

One of the most popular tourist attractions in California is Hollywood.
Hollywood has something for everyone.

LESSON F Another view

1 **Read the questions. Look at the amusement park information. Then fill in the correct answers.**

	Family Fun Amusement Park	Great Days Amusement Park
Admission	One-day adult admission $39.95 Junior (3–8) $29.95 Senior (55+) $32.95 Children under 3 are free	One-day adult admission $29.95 Junior (5–12) $19.95 Senior (65+) $24.95 Children under 5 are free
Amenities	Water rides and family rides Indoor and outdoor swimming pools 4 movie theaters Restaurants / cafés	Mini-golf and go-kart racing Climbing courses for all ages Child play center Restaurants / cafés
Restaurants	Price Range • Appetizers: $5.00–$7.50 • Main courses: $8.99–$15.00 • Desserts: $4.75–$7.50	Price Range • Appetizers: $5.00–$15.00 • Main courses: $12.00–$24.00 • Desserts: $5.50–$8.00
Driving distance from destinations	San Francisco, CA (2 hours) Los Angeles, CA (6 hours)	Boston, MA (4 hours) Washington, D.C. (5 hours)

1. What is the admission for a person aged 66 at Family Fun Amusement Park?
   - Ⓐ $24.95
   - Ⓑ $29.95
   - ● $32.95
   - Ⓓ $39.95

2. Which is the cheapest?
   - Ⓐ one junior admission at Family Fun
   - Ⓑ one junior admission at Great Days
   - Ⓒ one senior admission at Family Fun
   - Ⓓ one senior admission at Great Days

3. Which statement is true?
   - Ⓐ Children under five are free at Family Fun.
   - Ⓑ Children over three are free at Family Fun.
   - Ⓒ Children over three are free at Great Days.
   - Ⓓ Children under five are free at Great Days.

4. How far is Great Days from Boston?
   - Ⓐ 1.5 hours
   - Ⓑ 4 hours
   - Ⓒ 4.5 hours
   - Ⓓ 6 hours

5. Which statement is true?
   - Ⓐ Great Days has a child play center.
   - Ⓑ Great Days has a movie theater.
   - Ⓒ Family Fun has a climbing course.
   - Ⓓ Family Fun has mini-golf.

6. How much is the most expensive main course at Family Fun?
   - Ⓐ $8.99
   - Ⓑ $12.00
   - Ⓒ $15.00
   - Ⓓ $24.00

Check your answers. See page 141.

2 How do these sentences use the present perfect? Mark them A, B, or C as follows:

A = *events that begin in the past and continue until now*

B = *events that happened once in the past, time unclear*

C = *events that have been repeated in the past*

1. She's been to the Louvre Museum in Paris and has seen the Mona Lisa. __B__

2. I've already visited Alcatraz. I don't want to go again. _____

3. The Bradleys have been in Hawaii for two weeks. They'll be back tomorrow. _____

4. We're at the county fair. We've been on the Ferris wheel, and we've seen the fireworks. _____

5. I've read *The Lord of the Rings* four times. I'll probably read it again some day. _____

6. We've been standing in line to buy tickets to Sea Adventure for an hour now. _____

7. Jim said that he and his wife have eaten several meals at that restaurant, and they've all been good. _____

8. I know I've stayed at this hotel before, but I can't remember when. _____

3 Circle the best answer to complete the conversation.

1. **A** I've been to New York three times.

   B _____?

   (a.) Do you think you'll go again some day?

   b. How long have you been there?

2. **A** We've been in Peru for two weeks, but we haven't gone to Cuzco.

   B _____?

   a. Are you still in Peru?

   b. Will you go to Cuzco before you leave?

3. **A** I've visited Loch Ness in Scotland, but I didn't see the monster.

   B _____?

   a. When did you go there?

   b. How long have you been there?

4. **A** We're in Tokyo now.

   B _____?

   a. How long did you stay there?

   b. How long have you been there?

5. **A** We haven't been to Nova Scotia yet.

   B _____?

   a. When did you go there?

   b. Do you want to go?

6. **A** I've visited the museum more than once, but I haven't seen everything.

   B _____?

   a. How many times have you been there?

   b. How long have you been there?

Reference

Verbs + gerunds

A gerund is the base form of a verb + *-ing*. Gerunds often follow verbs that talk about preferences. Use a gerund like a noun: *I love dancing*.

Spelling rules for gerunds

- For verbs ending in a vowel-consonant pair, repeat the consonant before adding *-ing*:
  stop → stopping   *get → getting*
- For verbs ending in silent *-e*, drop the *e* before *-ing*:
  dance → dancing   *exercise → exercising*

  but:

  be → being   *see → seeing*

Questions

Do	I	
	you	enjoy dancing?
	we	
	they	
Does	he	
	she	
	it	

Affirmative statements

I		
You	enjoy	dancing.
We		
They		
He	enjoys	
She		
It		

Negative statements

I		
You	don't enjoy	dancing.
We		
They		
He	doesn't enjoy	
She		
It		

Verbs gerunds often follow

avoid	feel like	love	quit
can't help	finish	mind	recommend
dislike	hate	miss	regret
enjoy	like	practice	suggest

Gerunds after prepositions

Prepositions are words like *in*, *of*, *about*, and *for*. Prepositions are often used in phrases with adjectives (*excited about*, *interested in*) and verbs (*think about*). Gerunds often follow these phrases.

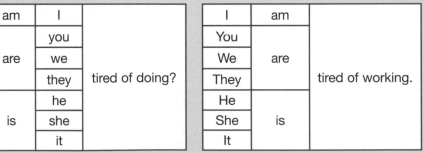

Wh- questions: *What*

What	am	I	
	are	you	tired of doing?
		we	
		they	
	is	he	
		she	
		it	

Affirmative statements

I	am	
You	are	tired of working.
We		
They		
He	is	
She		
It		

Phrases gerunds often follow

afraid of	famous for	nervous about	thank (someone) for
amazed by	good at	plan on	think about
angry at	happy about	pleased about	tired of
bad at	interested in	sad about	worried about
excited about	look forward to	talk about	

Verbs + infinitives

An infinitive is *to* + the base form of a verb. Infinitives often follow verbs that talk about future ideas. See below for a list of verbs that infinitives often follow.

Wh- questions: *Where*

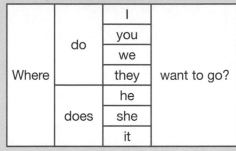

Where	do	I	want to go?
		you	
		we	
		they	
	does	he	
		she	
		it	

Affirmative statements

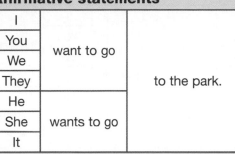

I	want to go	to the park.
You		
We		
They		
He	wants to go	
She		
It		

Yes / No questions

Do	I	want to go?
	you	
	we	
	they	
Does	he	
	she	
	it	

Short answers

Yes,	I	do.
	you	
	we	
	they	
	he	does.
	she	
	it	

No,	I	don't.
	you	
	we	
	they	
	he	doesn't.
	she	
	it	

don't = do not
doesn't = does not

Verbs infinitives often follow

agree	hope	need	promise
can / can't afford	intend	offer	refuse
decide	learn	plan	volunteer
expect	manage	prepare	want
help	mean	pretend	would like

Present perfect

The present perfect is *have* or *has* + past participle. Use the present perfect to talk about actions that started in the past and continue to now. See page 146 for a list of past participles with irregular verbs.

Use *how long* + present perfect to ask about length of time.
Use *for* with a period of time to answer questions with *how long*.
Use *since* with a point in time to answer questions with *how long*.

Wh- questions: *How long*

How long	have	I you we they	been	here?
	has	he she it	been	

Affirmative statements: *for* and *since*

I You We They	have been	here	for two hours. since 6:00 p.m.
He She It	has been		

Use *ever* with the present perfect to ask *Yes / No* questions about things that happened at any time before now.

haven't	=	have not
hasn't	=	has not

Yes / No questions: *ever*

Have	I you we they	ever	been late?
Has	he she it	ever	been late?

Short answers

Yes,	I you we they	have.
Yes,	he she it	has.

No,	I you we they	haven't.
No,	he she it	hasn't.

Use *recently* and *lately* with the present perfect to talk about things that happened in the very recent past, not very long ago.

Yes / No questions: *recently* and *lately*

Have	I you we they	been	early recently? early lately?
Has	he she it		

Use *already* and *yet* with the present perfect to talk about actions based on expectations.

Affirmative statements: *already*

I You We They	have	already	eaten.
He She It	has		

Negative statements: *yet*

I You We They	haven't	eaten	yet.
He She It	hasn't		

Present perfect continuous

The present perfect continuous is *have* or *has* + *been* + present participle. Use the present perfect continuous to talk about actions that started in the past, continue to now, and will probably continue in the future.

Yes / No questions

Have	I	been sitting here for a long time?
	you	
	we	
	they	
Has	he	
	she	
	it	

Short answers

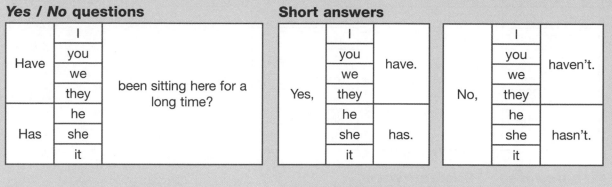

Yes,	I	have.
	you	
	we	
	they	
	he	has.
	she	
	it	

No,	I	haven't.
	you	
	we	
	they	
	he	hasn't.
	she	
	it	

Wh- questions: *How long*

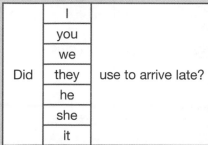

How long	have	I	been sitting here?
		you	
		we	
		they	
	has	he	
		she	
		it	

Affirmative statements: *for* and *since*

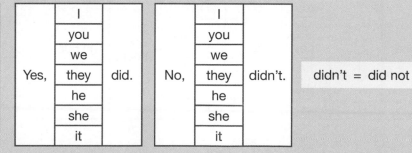

I	have been sitting here	for an hour.
You		since 10 a.m.
We		
They		
He	has been sitting here	
She		
It		

used to

Used to talks about things that happened in the past. Use *used to* to talk about a past situation or past habit that is not true now.

Yes / No questions

Did	I	use to arrive late?
	you	
	we	
	they	
	he	
	she	
	it	

Short answers

Yes,	I	did.
	you	
	we	
	they	
	he	
	she	
	it	

No,	I	didn't.
	you	
	we	
	they	
	he	
	she	
	it	

didn't = did not

Affirmative statements

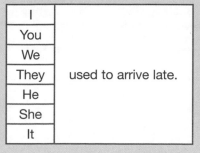

I	used to arrive late.
You	
We	
They	
He	
She	
It	

Past continuous

Use the past continuous to talk about actions that were happening at a specific time in the past. The actions were not completed at that time.

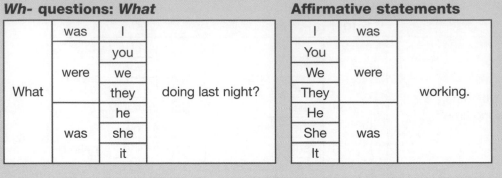

Wh- questions: *What*

What	was	I	doing last night?
	were	you	
		we	
		they	
	was	he	
		she	
		it	

Affirmative statements

I	was	working.
You	were	
We		
They		
He	was	
She		
It		

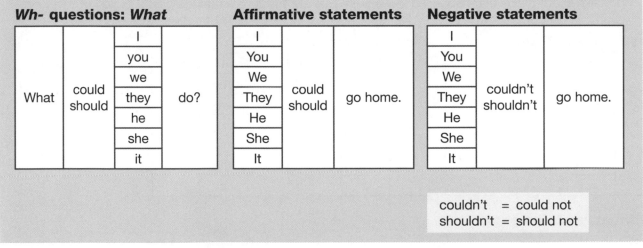

Yes / No questions

Was	I	working?
Were	you	
	we	
	they	
Was	he	
	she	
	it	

Short answers

Yes,	I	was.
	you	were.
	we	
	they	
	he	was.
	she	
	it	

No,	I	wasn't.
	you	weren't.
	we	
	they	
	he	wasn't.
	she	
	it	

wasn't = was not
weren't = were not

could and should

Use *could* to give suggestions. Use *should* to give advice. *Should* gives stronger advice than *could*.

Wh- questions: *What*

What	could should	I	do?
		you	
		we	
		they	
		he	
		she	
		it	

Affirmative statements

I	could should	go home.
You		
We		
They		
He		
She		
It		

Negative statements

I	couldn't shouldn't	go home.
You		
We		
They		
He		
She		
It		

couldn't = could not
shouldn't = should not

Irregular verbs

Base form	Simple past	Past participle	Base form	Simple past	Past participle
be	was / were	been	leave	left	left
become	became	become	lose	lost	lost
begin	began	begun	make	made	made
break	broke	broken	meet	met	met
bring	brought	brought	pay	paid	paid
build	built	built	put	put	put
buy	bought	bought	read	read	read
catch	caught	caught	ride	rode	ridden
choose	chose	chosen	run	ran	run
come	came	come	say	said	said
cost	cost	cost	see	saw	seen
cut	cut	cut	sell	sold	sold
do	did	done	send	sent	sent
drink	drank	drunk	set	set	set
drive	drove	driven	show	showed	shown
eat	ate	eaten	sing	sang	sung
fall	fell	fallen	sit	sat	sat
feel	felt	felt	sleep	slept	slept
fight	fought	fought	speak	spoke	spoken
find	found	found	spend	spent	spent
fly	flew	flown	stand	stood	stood
forget	forgot	forgotten	steal	stole	stolen
get	got	gotten / got	swim	swam	swum
give	gave	given	take	took	taken
go	went	gone	teach	taught	taught
have	had	had	tell	told	told
hear	heard	heard	think	thought	thought
hide	hid	hidden	throw	threw	thrown
hit	hit	hit	understand	understood	understood
hold	held	held	wake	woke	woken
hurt	hurt	hurt	wear	wore	worn
keep	kept	kept	win	won	won
know	knew	known	write	wrote	written

Spelling rules for regular past participles

- To form the past participle of regular verbs, add *-ed* to the base form:
  listen → *listened*

- For regular verbs ending in a consonant + *-y*, change *y* to *i* and add *-ed*:
  study → *studied*

- For regular verbs ending in a vowel + *-y*, add *-ed*:
  play → *played*

- For regular verbs ending in *-e*, add *-d*:
  live → *lived*

Grammar explanations

Separable phrasal verbs

A phrasal verb is a verb + preposition. The meaning of the phrasal verb is different from the meaning of the verb alone.

He *handed out* the papers to the class. = He *gave* the papers to the class.

A separable phrasal verb can have a noun between the verb and the preposition.

He *handed* **the papers** *out*.

A separable phrasal verb can have a pronoun between the verb and the preposition.

He *handed* **them** *out*.

Common separable phrasal verbs

call back	cut off	find out	look up	throw away / out
call up	do over	give back	pick out	turn down
clean up	fill in	hand in	put away / back	turn off
cross out	fill out	hand out	shut off	turn up
cut down	fill up	leave on	tear up	

Comparisons

Use *more than*, *less than*, and *as much as* to compare nouns and gerunds. A gerund is the base form of a verb + *-ing*. It is often used as a noun. You can compare activities by using gerunds and *more than*, *less than*, and *as much as*.

I enjoy *walking more than driving*.

She likes *cooking less than eating*.

They enjoy *singing as much as dancing*.

Giving reasons and explanations with *because of* phrases and *because* clauses

Use a *because of* phrase or a *because* clause to give an explanation. A *because of* phrase is the part of the sentence that begins with *because of* and has a noun phrase. A *because* clause is the part of the sentence that begins with *because* and has a subject and verb. Use a comma (,) when the *because of* phrase or *because* clause begins the sentence.

I came to Ohio *because of my children*.

Because of my children, I came to Ohio.

I came to Ohio *because my children are here*.

Because my children are here, I came to Ohio.

Adjectives with *too* and *enough*

Use *too* + adjective to talk about more than the right amount.

The ladder is *too tall*.

Use adjective + *enough* to talk about the right amount of something.

The ladder is *tall enough* to reach the ceiling.

Use *not* + adjective + *enough* to talk about less than the right amount.

The ladder is *not tall enough*.

Capitalization rules

Capitalize the first, last, and other important words in titles.	**M**y **S**trategies for **L**earning **E**nglish **S**alsa **S**tarz at **C**entury **P**ark **E**scape from **A**lcatraz
Capitalize letters in abbreviations.	**TV** (television) **DVD** (digital video disc or digital versatile disc) **ATM** (automated teller machine or automatic teller machine)
Capitalize titles when they follow a name.	Latisha Holmes, **P**resident, Rolling Hills Neighborhood Watch Janice Hill, **P**ersonnel **M**anager, Smart Shop

Adverb clauses

A clause is a part of a sentence that has a subject and a verb. A dependent clause often begins with time words such as *when*, *before*, and *after*. The dependent clause can come at the beginning or end of a sentence. Use a comma (,) after a dependent clause that comes at the beginning of a sentence. Do not use a comma when a dependent clause comes at the end of a sentence.

when: Use *when* + present time verbs to talk about habits.

> *When I have a lot to do*, I make a to-do list.
> I make a to-do list *when I have a lot to do*.

before: Use *before* to order events in a sentence. *Before* introduces the second event.

Use *before* with the simple present to talk about habits.

> First, she reads the newspaper. Second, she eats breakfast. =
> She reads the newspaper *before she eats breakfast*.
> *Before she eats breakfast*, she reads the newspaper.

Use *before* with the simple present and future to talk about future plans.

> First, he'll finish school. Second, he'll take a vacation. =
> He'll finish school *before he takes a vacation*.
> *Before he takes a vacation*, he'll finish school.

after: Use *after* to order events in a sentence. *After* introduces the first event.

Use *after* with the simple present to talk about habits.

> First, I eat dinner. Second, I watch the news. =
> I watch the news *after I eat dinner*.
> *After I eat dinner*, I watch the news.

Use *after* with the simple present and future to talk about future plans.

> First, he'll finish school. Second, he'll take a vacation. =
> He'll take a vacation *after he finishes school*.
> *After he finishes school*, he'll take a vacation.

when and **while**: Use *when* or *while* with the past continuous and simple past to show that one past action interrupted another past action.

Use *when* with the simple past for the action that interrupted.

> They were sleeping *when the fire started*.
> *When the fire started*, they were sleeping.

Use *while* with the past continuous to show the action that was happening before the interruption.

> The fire started *while they were sleeping*.
> *While they were sleeping*, the fire started.

if: Use *if* clauses to talk about future possibility. Use the simple present in the clause with *if*. Use the future in the other clause to talk about what could happen.

> She won't go *if the weather is bad*.
> *If the weather is bad*, she won't go.

Answer key

Welcome

Exercise 1 page 2
1. c 2. b 3. b 4. a 5. b 6. a

Exercise 2 page 3
1. wants to get
2. needs to improve
3. needs to take
4. needs to get
5. needs to apply
6. wants to work

Exercise 3 page 3
1. Emile wants to open a men's clothing store.
2. He needs to find a good location for the store.
3. Farah and Ali want to study engineering in college.
4. They need to take a lot of math classes.
5. Monica wants to pass the GED exam.
6. She needs to take some special classes.
7. Adrian wants to buy a new car.
8. He needs to save his money.

Exercise 4 page 4
1. is   5. puts, checks
2. is living   6. wants
3. has   7. goes
4. is working   8. is learning

Exercise 5 page 4
1. At the moment, Miguel is living with his brother Tony.
2. Tony has a job at a computer store.
3. Right now he is working as a salesperson.
4. He wants to become a computer technician.
5. Tony is taking English classes every Thursday evening.
6. Tony and Miguel are studying English together now.

Exercise 6 page 5
1. came   5. decided
2. wanted   6. will start
3. played   7. liked
4. began   8. will teach

Exercise 7 page 5
1. did you come to this country
2. did you come to this country
3. did you play for
4. did you play for them
5. did you decide to change your career plan
6. will you start your new job
7. will you teach
8. will you stay here

Unit 1: Personal information

Lesson A: Listening

Exercise 1 page 6
1. a 2. c 3. b 4. c 5. a 6. c

Exercise 2 page 7
1. outgoing   4. dislikes
2. enjoys   5. shy
3. going out   6. alone

Exercise 3 page 7
1. dislikes   4. dislikes
2. enjoys   5. dislikes
3. enjoys

Exercise 4 page 7
1. outgoing   3. stay home
2. quiet   4. dislike

Exercise 5 page 7
reading books, fixing old cars, listening to music, talking about movies

Lesson B: Verbs + gerunds

Exercise 1 page 8
1. getting up early
2. doing homework
3. doing homework
4. playing soccer
5. playing soccer
6. getting up early

Exercise 2 page 8
1. Yes, he does.
2. No, she doesn't.
3. No, he doesn't.
4. Yes, they do.
5. No, he doesn't.
6. No, he doesn't.

Exercise 3 page 9
1. going out   5. listening
2. being   6. doing
3. working   7. playing
4. reading   8. surfing

Exercise 4 page 9
1A. going out
1B. Yes, he does.
2A. being
2B. Yes, he does.
3A. reading
3B. No, he doesn't.
4A. doing
4B. No, he doesn't.

Exercise 5 page 9
1. Do you enjoy going to the beach?
2. Do you dislike standing in line?
3. Do you like playing cards?
4. Do you mind taking out the garbage?

Lesson C: Comparisons

Exercise 1 page 10
1. playing sports
2. socializing with friends
3. dancing
4. cooking
5. watching movies
6. reading

Exercise 2 page 10
1. Angelina likes watching movies less than cooking.
2. Angelina likes watching movies more than reading.
3. Angelina likes cooking less than dancing.
4. Angelina likes socializing with friends more than dancing.
5. Angelina likes playing sports as much as socializing with friends.

Exercise 3 page 11
1. Ling likes painting more than playing an instrument.
2. Frank enjoys riding a bicycle more than driving a car.
3. Suzanna enjoys reading more than washing the dishes.
4. Annie and Steve like going to the movies more than shopping.

Exercise 4 page 11
1. Annie and Steve like shopping less <u>than</u> watching movies.
2. Ling likes playing an instrument <u>less</u> than painting.
3. Suzanna enjoys washing dishes less <u>than</u> reading.
4. Frank enjoys riding a bike <u>more</u> than driving a car.

Lesson D: Reading

Exercise 1 page 12
1. architect
2. computer programmer
3. teacher

Exercise 2 page 12
1. architect
2. computer programmer
3. teacher
4. computer programmer
5. teacher
6. architect

Exercise 3 page 13
Computer programmers: find answers to problems, like working alone
Teachers: help students, like learning about people
Architects: design new homes, imagine new ideas

Exercise 4 page 13
1. personality   5. friendly
2. intellectual   6. type
3. creative   7. outgoing
4. artist

Lesson E: Writing

Exercise 1 page 14
Jobs: architect, designer, scientist, social worker, teacher
Personality adjectives: creative, friendly, helpful, outgoing, reliable
Activities: drawing, finding answers, helping people, surfing the Internet, talking

Exercise 2 page 14
Name: Peter Jones
Job: social worker
Place of work: community center
Personality: friendly and outgoing
Likes: meeting and helping people

Exercise 3 page 15
1. computer programmer
2. intellectual
3. hardworking
4. finding answers

Exercise 4 page 15
Answer may vary.

Lesson F: Another view
Exercise 1 page 16
1. C   2. A   3. A   4. D   5. C   6. B

Exercise 2 page 17
1. c; Ruben must be a little shy.
2. a; Miguel must love music.
3. d; Adriana must be very intelligent.
4. a; Hana must like sports a lot.

Exercise 3 page 17
1. She must not be a very good cook.
2. He must be very creative.
3. He must not be a reliable employee.
4. She must not like working out.
5. She must know how to swim.

Unit 2: At school
Lesson A: Listening
Exercise 1 page 18
1. paper   4. index cards
2. list   5. concentrate
3. underline   6. discouraged

Exercise 2 page 18
1. b   2. c   3. b   4. a

Exercise 3 page 19
1. d   2. a   3. f   4. e   5. b   6. c

Exercise 4 page 19
1. list   5. underline
2. paper   6. index cards
3. concentrate   7. boring
4. active   8. discouraged

Exercise 5 page 19
Bad study habits: doesn't study new words, is late for class, hands in homework late, forgets homework, doesn't study for tests
Good study habits: makes to-do lists, writes new words on index cards, underlines the main ideas

Exercise 6 page 19
Mr. Wilson has talked about learning strategies in class.

Lesson B: Present perfect
Exercise 1 page 20
1. for   5. since
2. since   6. since
3. since   7. for
4. for   8. since

Exercise 2 page 20
1. have   4. have
2. have   5. has
3. has   6. have

Exercise 3 page 20
1. has worked   4. has had
2. have lived   5. has taught
3. have studied   6. has been

Exercise 4 page 21
1A. has he been
1B. four hours, 3:00 p.m.
2A. has she known
2B. four months, August 1
3A. has he lived
3B. two years, June 25, 2011

Exercise 5 page 21
1. have they worked in this school
2. has she had a driver's license
3. has he lived in this apartment
4. have you been married

Lesson C: Present perfect
Exercise 1 page 22
1. lost   4. taken
2. forgotten   5. gotten
3. read

Exercise 2 page 22
1A. Has, studied
1B. Yes, she has.
2A. Have, talked
2B. No, they haven't.
3A. Has, made
3B. Yes, she has.
4A. Have, written
4B. Yes, they have.
5A. Has, done
5B. No, he hasn't.

Exercise 3 page 23
1. Have you ever used
2. Has your teacher ever talked
3. Have your friends ever studied
4. Have you ever written
5. Have you ever underlined
6. Have you ever gotten

Exercise 4 page 23
1. Melissa hasn't ever forgotten to study for a test. She has lost her textbook.
2. Franco has had trouble concentrating on his homework. He hasn't ever done the wrong homework.
3. Rose has read the newspaper in English. She hasn't ever tried to speak English with her neighbors.

Lesson D: Reading
Exercise 1 page 24
1. The article is about strategies for learning new words.
2. 1. Keep a vocabulary notebook.
   2. Make vocabulary cards.
   3. Use new words in conversations every day.
3. Make vocabulary cards.

Exercise 2 page 25
1. b   2. d   3. a   4. b

Exercise 3 page 25
1. c   2. d   3. e   4. a   5. b

Exercise 4 page 25
1. strategies
2. set
3. plan
4. practice
5. clues
6. gestures

Lesson E: Writing
Exercise 1 page 26
Listening strategies: Listen to the radio. Watch movies in English. Watch the news in English
Speaking strategies: Ask questions in class every day. Talk to people at work in English. Use new words in everyday conversation.
Reading strategies: Look up new words in a dictionary. Read newspapers in English. Underline new words with colored pens.

Exercise 2 page 26
1. Omar's first strategy is to read newspapers or magazines in English. He is going to read a newspaper article in English every day.

2. Omar's second strategy is to use colored pens to underline new words. He is going to use a yellow pen for new and difficult words. He is going to use a blue pen when he can guess the meaning of words.
3. Omar's third strategy is to use his dictionary more often. He is going to choose five words he doesn't know each day and check their meanings.

Exercise 3 page 27
1. 4   2. 2   3. 3   4. 1

Exercise 4 page 27
Answer may vary.

Lesson F: Another view
Exercise 1 page 28
1. Read   5. worry
2. Skim   6. Make
3. Answer   7. look
4. spend

Exercise 2 page 28
1. 4   2. 5   3. 6   4. 7   5. 2   6. 3   7. 1

Exercise 3 page 29
1. has been
2. has always gotten
3. have gone
4. had
5. needed
6. started
7. has worked
8. talked
9. gave
10. have improved

Exercise 4 page 29
1. Has Tran ever forgotten to put his name on a test?
Yes. He forgot to put his name on a history test last week.
2. Has Naomi ever watched a TV show in English?
Yes. She watched the news on the BBC last night.
3. Have Naomi and Tran ever studied geometry?
Yes. They studied geometry in the first year of high school.

Unit 3: Friends and family
Lesson A: Listening
Exercise 1 page 30
1. came over   4. borrow
2. favor   5. noisy
3. broken   6. complain

Exercise 2 page 30
1. a   2. b   3. d   4. a

Exercise 3 page 31
1. borrow   5. complained
2. noisy   6. noise
3. appreciates   7. favor
4. owe   8. come over

Exercise 4 page 31
1. lent   3. borrowed
2. borrowed   4. lent

Exercise 5 page 31
1. lend   3. borrow
2. lend   4. borrow

Exercise 6 page 31
He's going to borrow a key from the building manager.

Lesson B: Phrases and clauses with *because*

Exercise 1 page 32
1. c   2. a   3. e   4. b   5. d

Exercise 2 page 32
1. because
2. because
3. because of
4. because of
5. because of
6. because

Exercise 3 page 32
1. We couldn't sleep because of the noise.
2. We couldn't play soccer because of the rain.
3. They were late for the appointment because of the traffic.
4. Reyna stayed at home because of the flu.
5. Sam stayed up late because of the basketball game.
6. Beatriz moved to this country because of her children.

Exercise 4 page 33
1. because
2. because
3. because of
4. because of
5. because

Exercise 5 page 33
1. because it was closed
2. because of the rain
3. because it was her son's birthday
4. because of the smoke
5. because he was sick
6. because there were so many people

Lesson C: Adverbs of degree

Exercise 1 page 34
1. hot
2. tall
3. small
4. strong
5. close
6. young

Exercise 2 page 34
1. hot
2. tall
3. strong
4. small
5. young
6. close

Exercise 3 page 34
1. too young
2. old enough
3. too weak
4. strong enough
5. too small
6. big enough

Exercise 4 page 35
1A. too noisy
1B. not quiet enough
2A. too expensive
2B. not cheap enough
3A. too small
3B. not big enough
4A. too difficult
4B. not easy enough
5A. too boring
5B. not interesting enough
6A. too young
6B. not old enough

Exercise 5 page 35
1. big enough
2. tall enough
3. old enough
4. too high
5. strong enough
6. too young
7. experienced enough
8. too expensive
9. too weak

Lesson D: Reading

Exercise 1 page 36
1. The writer gets together with her neighbors once a month.
2. Some teenagers painted the graffiti.
3. The writer's neighbors shouted at the teenagers, and they ran away.
4. The writer's neighborhood is safe.

Exercise 2 page 37
1. c   2. a   3. b   4. d

Exercise 3 page 37
1. get into
2. get together
3. look after
4. goes off
5. run away
6. break into

Exercise 4 page 37
1. run away
2. look after
3. get together
4. goes off
5. get into
6. break into

Lesson E: Writing

Exercise 1 page 38
1. today's date
2. problem
3. request
4. signature

Exercise 2 page 38
1. F
2. F
3. F
4. T
5. T
6. T
7. F
8. T

Exercise 3 page 39
1. soon
2. because
3. too
4. advance
5. because of

Exercise 4 page 39
Answer may vary.

Lesson F: Another view

Exercise 1 page 40
1. A   2. C   3. C   4. B   5. B   6. B

Exercise 2 page 41
1. aren't / are not able to do
2. are able to
3. aren't / are not able to have
4. 's / is able to open
5. isn't / is not able to fix
6. isn't / is not able to be
7. 're / are able to rent
8. 'm / am not able to leave

Exercise 3 page 41
1. I'm (not) able to run a mile in 10 minutes.
2. I'm (not) able to lift 50 pounds with one hand.
3. I'm (not) able to speak Japanese.
4. I'm (not) able to play the piano for my classmates.
5. I'm (not) able to fix a computer.
6. I'm (not) able to change a flat tire.

Unit 4: Health

Lesson A: Listening

Exercise 1 page 42
1. diet
2. exercise
3. pressure
4. gained
5. weight
6. advice

Exercise 2 page 42
1. a   2. b   3. b   4. b

Exercise 3 page 43
Healthy activities: check your weight, eat breakfast, eat fish, ride a bicycle,
Unhealthy activities: drink a lot of soda, eat a lot of hamburgers, gain 20 pounds, go to bed late

Exercise 4 page 43
1. diet
2. medication
3. weight
4. exercise
5. advice

Exercise 5 page 43
Past: eat fast food for lunch; take the elevator; work 12 hours a day;
Now: have soup for lunch; walk up the stairs; eat breakfast; go to the gym; leave work at 5:30

Lesson B: Present perfect

Exercise 1 page 44
1. have gained
2. have given
3. have not eaten
4. have started
5. have exercised
6. has gone
7. have not been

Exercise 2 page 44
1. You haven't exercised this week.
2. Paul has gained weight recently.
3. Ray and Louisa have lost weight recently.
4. Alicia has been unhappy lately.
5. My blood pressure has gone up recently.
6. Greg hasn't visited a dentist recently.
7. Sarah has given up desserts lately.

Exercise 3 page 45
1. Annette hasn't checked her blood pressure recently.
2. Annette has gone to the gym recently.
3. Annette has eaten more fruits and vegetables recently.
4. Annette has slept eight hours a day recently.
5. Annette hasn't taken vitamins recently.

Exercise 4 page 45
1A. Has Bill lost weight recently?
1B. he hasn't.
2A. Have Tina and Mario given up desserts recently?
2B. they have.
3A. Have you checked your blood pressure lately?
3B. I haven't.
4A. Has Barbara slept much lately?
4B. she has.
5A. Has Lisa started taking vitamins recently?
5B. she hasn't.

Lesson C: *Used to*

Exercise 1 page 46
1. use
2. used
3. used
4. use
5. used
6. use

Exercise 2 page 46
1. used to
2. use to
3. used to
4. used to
5. use to
6. used to

Exercise 3 page 46
1. used to eat
2. eats
3. takes
4. used to exercise
5. goes
6. used to drive
7. rides
8. used to drink
9. drinks
10. used to feel
11. has

Exercise 4 page 47

1. Emilia used to stay up until 2:00 a.m., but now she goes to bed at 10:00 p.m.
2. Emilia used to eat meat every day, but now she eats fish twice a week.
3. Emilia used to go straight home after work, but now she goes to the gym three times a week.
4. Emilia used to eat a lot of fatty foods, but now she eats salad and vegetables.
5. Emilia used to skip breakfast, but now she eats fruit and yogurt for breakfast.

Exercise 5 page 47

1A. Did Emilia use to stay up until 2:00 a.m.?
1B. Yes, she did.
2A. Did Emilia use to eat meat every day?
2B. Yes, she did.
3A. Did Emilia use to go to the gym three times a week?
3B. No, she didn't.

Lesson D: Reading
Exercise 1 page 48

1. Mint is good for treating indigestion.
2. Lavender is good for treating headaches.
3. Mint is good for treating stomachaches.
4. Thyme tea can help treat a cough or a sore throat.

Exercise 2 page 49

Thyme: Use it to make tea. Use it to cook chicken and fish. Use it to treat a cough and sore throat.
Lavender: Use it to make tea. Use it to cook meat. Use it to treat headaches and high blood pressure.
Mint: Use it to make tea. Use it to cook meat and fish. Use it to treat indigestion and upset stomachs.

Exercise 3 page 49

1. digestion	4. herbal
2. treatment	5. digest
3. prevent	6. treat

Exercise 4 page 49

1. adjective	5. verb
2. noun	6. verb
3. verb or noun	7. noun
4. noun	

Lesson E: Writing
Exercise 1 page 50

1. cooking and medicine
2. green-gray leaves and purple flowers
3. sore throats and breathing problems
4. to add flavor to meat and vegetables
5. as a mouthwash

Exercise 2 page 50

1. Rosemary
2. garden or in your home
3. sharp, narrow leaves
4. headaches
5. add flavor to meat or oil

Exercise 3 page 51

1. in hot, dry places
2. long, spiky leaves with juice inside
3. burns, insect bites, and dry skin
4. skin creams and lotions, shampoos, and soaps

Exercise 4 page 51

Answer may vary.

Lesson F: Another view
Exercise 1 page 52

1. B   2. D   3. D   4. C

Exercise 2 page 53

1. Dr. Chang told Harry Johnson not to eat sweets between meals.
2. He also told him to try to get more exercise.
3. Alec's mother told him to take his vitamins.
4. His father told him not to stay out late every night.
5. Ms. Bailey told the class not to stay up late studying for the test.
6. She also told them to eat a good breakfast in the morning.
7. Magda told Helen to use mint leaves to make iced tea.
8. Then she told her not to put too much sugar in it.

Unit 5: Around town
Lesson A: Listening
Exercise 1 page 54

1. B   2. D   3. C   4. A

Exercise 2 page 54

1. events	4. admission
2. concerts	5. storytelling
3. afford	6. exhibits

Exercise 3 page 55

1. d	3. d	5. b
2. c	4. b	6. c

Exercise 4 page 55

go to a museum, go out for coffee

Lesson B: Verbs + infinitives
Exercise 1 page 56

1. to go	4. to eat
2. to see	5. to take
3. to meet	6. to come home

Exercise 2 page 56

1. want to ride
2. plans to eat
3. intends to meet
4. need to take
5. she expects to be
6. would like to buy
7. hopes to find

Exercise 3 page 57

1. Tony promises to visit his family every year.
2. Lee expects to finish work early tonight.
3. I plan to go to Florida this winter.
4. Shin intends to buy some concert tickets tomorrow.
5. We hope to visit our daughter in California next month.
6. Paul refuses to go to the beach this weekend.
7. I want to meet my friends on my birthday.
8. I would like to take a trip with my family next year.

Exercise 4 page 57

1. Chris plans to watch less TV.
2. Chris intends to go to an art museum.
3. Chris wants to visit relatives more often.
4. Chris plans to walk to work every day.
5. Chris would like to give up desserts.
6. Chris hopes to buy organic vegetables.

Lesson C: Present perfect
Exercise 1 page 58

1. seen	4. paid
2. made	5. bought
3. read	6. done

Exercise 2 page 58

1. hasn't started yet
2. has already closed
3. has already ended
4. hasn't opened yet

Exercise 3 page 59

1. Has, brought / Yes, he has.
2. Has, invited / Yes, she has.
3. Has, gotten / No, he hasn't.
4. Has, baked / No, she hasn't
5. Has, bought / Yes, he has.
6. Have, put up / Yes, they have.
7. Have, set up / No, they haven't.

Exercise 4 page 59

1. We haven't gone to the park <u>yet</u>.
2. Our favorite TV show hasn't <u>started</u> yet.
3. Have <u>you</u> bought tickets for the fund-raiser yet?
4. They <u>haven't</u> eaten lunch yet.
5. Ivan and Alex <u>have</u> already been to that restaurant.
6. <u>Has</u> Julie visited the art exhibit yet?

Lesson D: Reading
Exercise 1 page 60

1. F   2. F   3. F   4. T   5. T   6. F   7. T

Exercise 2 page 61

1. d   2. d   3. b   4. d   5. b

Exercise 3 page 61

1. We missed the concert.
2. The concert was superb.
3. There was a crowd.
4. The waiting time was excessive.
5. There were five musicians.
6. The stage was unremarkable.

Lesson E: Writing
Exercise 1 page 62

Positive: amazing, fabulous, incredible, superb
Negative: excessive, irritating, ominous, unremarkable

Exercise 2 page 62

Positive adjectives: fabulous, incredible, amazing
Negative adjectives: terrible, irritating, unremarkable

Exercise 3 page 63

1. b, N	4. c, P
2. a, N	5. d, N
3. e, N	

Exercise 4 page 63

Answer may vary.

Lesson F: Another view
Exercise 1 page 64

1. A   2. C   3. D   4. C   5. B   6. D

Exercise 2 page 65

1. reading	5. listening
2. to go	6. to see
3. to buy	7. walking
4. being	8. to study

Exercise 3 page 65

1. Betty prefers going to crafts fairs, not to the mall.
2. x

3. The lights went out, but the musicians continued to play.
4. x
5. I started to read the book last night, and I've already finished it.
6. x
7. x
8. Raul hates driving in the city during rush hour.

Unit 6: Time

Lesson A: Listening

Exercise 1 page 66
1. chores
2. deadline
3. due
4. tasks
5. procrastinating
6. prioritize
7. impatient

Exercise 2 page 66
1. to-do list
2. procrastinating
3. chores
4. due
5. prioritize
6. impatient

Exercise 3 page 67
1. a 3. b 5. b
2. b 4. c 6. a

Exercise 4 page 67
1. b 2. e 3. d 4. c 5. a

Exercise 5 page 67
2. Alicia has learned to manage her time.
3. Thomas often procrastinates.

Lesson B: Adverb clauses

Exercise 1 page 68
1. b 3. a 5. c
2. e 4. f 6. d

Exercise 2 page 68
1. When Parvana has a lot of homework, she makes a to-do list of her tasks.
2. When she wants to concentrate, she goes to the library.
3. She looks at the clock when she starts her work.
4. When she finishes a task, she checks it off her to-do list.
5. She takes a short break when she feels tired.
6. When she doesn't hand in her homework on time, her teacher is upset.
7. She eats a snack when she feels hungry.
8. When she needs to focus, she doesn't answer the phone.
9. She does the difficult tasks first when she has a lot of work to do.
10. When she has a deadline, she doesn't procrastinate.

Exercise 3 page 69
1. When I finish my homework, I take a break.
2. no comma
3. no comma
4. When we don't hand in our homework, our teacher is very upset.
5. When I have a deadline, I stay up late.
6. no comma

Exercise 4 page 69
1A. What do you do when you finish a difficult task?
1B. I take a break.
2A. What do you do when you need to concentrate?
2B. I go to the library.
3A. What do you do when you don't understand the homework?
3B. I ask my teacher.
4A. What do you do when you have a quiz or a test?
4B. I study my notes.
5A. What do you do when you feel tired?
5B. I rest.
6A. What do you do when you don't want to work?
6B. I procrastinate.

Lesson C: Adverb clauses

Exercise 1 page 70
1. after he wakes up
2. after he gets dressed
3. after he eats breakfast
4. after he works out
5. after he takes a shower

Exercise 2 page 70
1. Janet gets home before she eats dinner.
2. Janet eats dinner before she walks the dog.
3. Janet walks the dog before she watches TV.
4. Janet watches TV before she reads a book.

Exercise 3 page 71
1A. What does Mannie do before he eats breakfast?
1B. He gets dressed.
2A. What does Mannie do before he works out?
2B. He eats breakfast.
3A. What does Mannie do before he goes to work?
3B. He takes a shower.
4A. What does Janet do after she gets home?
4B. She eats dinner.
5A. What does Janet do after she watches TV?
5B. She reads a book.
6A. What does Janet do after she reads a book?
6B. She goes to bed.

Exercise 4 page 71
1. I watch TV after I have dinner.
2. Before Sandy goes to work, she buys a newspaper.
3. Ivana goes to school after she finishes work.
4. After Simon finishes his homework, he takes a break.
5. They usually go swimming after they go to the park.
6. Before you go out, you need to take out the trash.
7. Melanie puts on makeup after she takes a shower.
8. Alan washes the dishes before he goes to bed.

Lesson D: Reading

Exercise 1 page 72
1. c 2. a 3. b 4. d

Exercise 2 page 73
1. impolite
2. impatient
3. punctuality
4. irresponsible
5. uncommon

Exercise 3 page 73
1. It is uncommon to miss a plane.
2. It is impolite to be late.
3. It is unusual to be early for a party.
4. He is impatient.
5. They are irresponsible.
6. She is disorganized.

Exercise 4 page 73
1. lucky
2. possible
3. honest
4. friendly
5. kind
6. rational

Lesson E: Writing

Exercise 1 page 74
1. Nita is a very organized person.
2. She keeps all of her class notes in one binder with different sections.
3. She writes all of her homework assignments and due dates in a special notebook.
4. In summary

Exercise 2 page 74
1. She writes all her homework assignments and due dates in a special notebook.
2. She keeps all her notes in one binder with different sections.
3. She checks her bag carefully and makes sure she has all the books she needs.
4. She plans how much time she will need for each assignment.
5. She takes a short break.

Exercise 3 page 75
My boss Frida is a very impatient person. For example, she often gets angry when you are three minutes late. She is also not a good listener, and she often interrupts. Finally, she is always in a hurry and never has enough time. In conclusion, Frida is a very impatient person, and it is difficult to work for her.

Exercise 4 page 75
Answer may vary.

Lesson F: Another view

Exercise 1 page 76
1. C 2. D 3. C 4. B 5. A

Exercise 2 page 77
1. it
2. them
3. one
4. it's
5. some
6. one

Exercise 3 page 77
1. Yes, I've memorized one. / No, I haven't memorized one.
2. Yes, I've seen it. / No, I haven't seen it.
3. Yes, I've made one. / No, I haven't made one.
4. Yes, I circled them. / No, I didn't circle them.
5. Yes, I have one. / No, I don't have one.
6. Yes, I visit them. / No, I don't visit them.

Unit 7: Shopping

Lesson A: Listening

Exercise 1 page 78
1. d   2. d   3. c   4. b

Exercise 2 page 79
1. afford   4. interest
2. credit   5. pay off
3. cash   6. balance

Exercise 3 page 79
1. $2,500.00
2. $250.00
3. $500.00

Exercise 4 page 79
1. $2,500   3. $100
2. 24   4. $550

Lesson B: Modals

Exercise 1 page 80
1. b   2. e   3. d   4. f   5. c   6. a

Exercise 2 page 80
1. buy   4. talk
2. taking   5. apply
3. use   6. looking

Exercise 3 page 80
1. should   4. should
2. could   5. could
3. should   6. should

Exercise 4 page 81
1. using your credit card
2. buy a used one
3. buy a new one
4. walking more often
5. looking for a cheaper plan
6. open a savings account

Exercise 5 page 81
1. should we do
2. should I tell
3. should I buy
4. should I make
5. should I wear

Lesson C: Gerunds after prepositions

Exercise 1 page 82
1. applying   7. losing
2. being   8. making
3. buying   9. opening
4. finding   10. paying
5. getting   11. studying
6. lending   12. waiting

Exercise 2 page 82
1. waiting   4. opening
2. buying   5. studying
3. applying   6. getting

Exercise 3 page 83
1. about   4. about
2. about   5. for
3. of

Exercise 4 page 83
1. about finding a job
2. for driving me to work
3. about getting a scholarship
4. of getting up early
5. of losing their jobs
6. in learning about computers

Exercise 5 page 83
1. Ron is excited about going to college.
2. Miguel is afraid of losing his job.
3. Vincent and Anna are happy about paying off their loan.

4. Tim and Betsy are worried about getting into debt.
5. Steve is interested in buying a new car.

Lesson D: Reading

Exercise 1 page 84
1. They can't afford the minimum payments.
2. They offer a 10–15 percent discount.
3. You won't have to pay any interest.
4. They say you should have at least two cards.

Exercise 2 page 85
1. Choose credit cards with low interest rates.
2. Keep the account balance low.
3. Always try to pay more than just the minimum payment.
4. Have no more than six cards.

Exercise 3 page 85
1. e   2. a   3. d   4. c   5. b

Exercise 4 page 85
1. credit   4. minimum
2. interest   5. counselor
3. budget

Exercise 5 page 85
1. interest rate
2. family budget
3. credit card
4. debt counselor
5. minimum payment

Lesson E: Writing

Exercise 1 page 86
1. c   2. d   3. b   4. a

Exercise 2 page 86
1. Gas is very expensive. His car uses a lot of gas. He needs to see an auto mechanic for repairs. He is worried about having his car break down.
2. Ask a co-worker to give you a ride to work and share the cost of gas. Drive to work three times a week and take the bus twice a week. Take the bus for a couple of months and save money.

Exercise 4 page 87
Answer may vary.

Lesson F: Another view

Exercise 1 page 88
1. A   2. C   3. B   4. B   5. A   6. D

Exercise 2 page 89
1. took   5. take
2. gets   6. take
3. got   7. get
4. takes   8. getting

Exercise 3 page 89
1. You should always take notes during class.
2. Milos and Judy were married, but last month they got divorced.
3. I'm tired. I'm going to take a nap.
4. Harriet used to work for the phone company, but she got fired last week.
5. It takes Lucy an hour to get dressed.
6. I'm going to take a trip next month.

Unit 8: Work

Lesson A: Listening

Exercise 1 page 90
1. employed   5. degree
2. strengths   6. personnel
3. reliable   7. shift
4. gets along

Exercise 2 page 90
1. reservations clerk
2. Senegal
3. cashier
4. computer, copy machine, and fax machine
5. responsible and friendly

Exercise 3 page 91
1. I'm from Senegal.
2. I'm a cashier in a pharmacy.
3. I can use a computer, a copy machine, and a fax machine.
4. I speak French fluently and English very well.
5. Yes, I am going to college to get a degree in hotel management.
6. I am reliable and friendly.

Exercise 4 page 91
1. get along   4. interview
2. employed   5. shift
3. strengths   6. background

Exercise 5 page 91
1. building manager
2. Argentina
3. custodian
4. hard-working

Lesson B: Present perfect continuous

Exercise 1 page 92
for: a long time, one hour, three months, two weeks
since: September, Tuesday, 2:00 p.m., 2005
all: day, morning, week, year

Exercise 2 page 92
1. Kendra has been working in the library since October.
2. Frank and Marta have been studying computers for two years.
3. Carla has been looking for a job since January.
4. I have been waiting for an interview since 1:30 p.m.
5. You have been talking on the phone for two hours.
6. We have been using the library computers all morning.
7. Kemal has been driving a cab for 20 years.
8. Gloria has been cooking food all day.

Exercise 3 page 93
1A. How long have Alicia and Claire been painting the house?
1B. Since 11:00 a.m.
    For 30 minutes.
2A. How long has Inez been cooking?
2B. Since 4:00 p.m.
    For two hours.
3A. How long have Tony and Leon been studying computers?
3B. Since June 1st.
    For one month.
4A. How long has Yoshi been working in the hotel?
4B. Since Tuesday.
    For five days.

5A. How long have you been using a
   computer?
5B. Since August.
   For three months.
6A. How long has Lenka been driving?
6B. Since 10:00 a.m.
   For three hours.
7A. How long has Juan been attending
   this school?
7B. Since January.
   For three weeks.

Lesson C: Phrasal verbs
Exercise 1 page 94
1. back	4. up
2. out	5. away
3. down	

Exercise 2 page 94
1. needs to turn it down
2. is cleaning it up
3. is throwing them away
4. are putting them away
5. need to call him back

Exercise 3 page 94
1. them away	4. it up
2. it up	5. it out
3. him back	

Exercise 4 page 95
1. I don't have time to call him back.
2. Please throw it out.
3. Please put them away.
4. Let's turn it on.

Exercise 5 page 95
1. She's putting away her clothes.
   She's putting her clothes away.
   She's putting them away.

2. He's handing out the tests.
   He's handing the tests out.
   He's handing them out.

3. She's cleaning up her kitchen
   She's cleaning her kitchen up.
   She's cleaning it up.

4. He's calling back Doctor Kim.
   He's calling Doctor Kim back.
   He's calling him back.

Lesson D: Reading
Exercise 1 page 96
1. Ivan wrote the blog.
2. The blog is about Ivan's new job.
3. Ivan has been writing the blog for
   five days.
4. He asks readers to share tips with him
   about starting a new job.

Exercise 2 page 97
5, 2, 4, 1, 6, 3

Exercise 3 page 97
1. d	4. b
2. a	5. c
3. e	

Exercise 4 page 97
1. a	3. a	5. b
2. b	4. b	6. b

Exercise 5 page 97
1. confidence	4. patience
2. excitement	5. depression
3. seriousness	

Lesson E: Writing
Exercise 1 page 98
                        264 West Street
                        Minneapolis, MN 55404
                        August 15, 2013
Ms. Ann Robinson
Office Manager
City Office Services
2321 Central Avenue
Minneapolis, MN 55409

Dear Ms. Robinson:
I would like to thank you for the job
interview I had with you on August 14th.
I appreciate the time you spent with me.
I enjoyed seeing the office and learning
more about the company.
Thank you again for your time. I hope to
hear from you soon.
Sincerely,
Sarah Bonarelli

Exercise 2 page 99
Answer may vary.

Lesson F: Another view
Exercise 1 page 100
1. B	2. B	3. D	4. D	5. C	6. A

Exercise 2 page 101
1. Eliza's reading a mystery story
   She's been reading

2. The Jensens are living in Miami
   They've been living

3. I'm studying Russian
   I've been studying

4. Esteban is looking for a job
   He's been looking for a job

5. Jun is organizing his papers
   He's been organizing

6. Julie is writing her blog
   She's been writing

Exercise 3 page 101
1. has been working
2. 's / has been feeling
3. 's / has been looking
4. 's / is planning
5. 's / is writing
6. 's / reading
7. 've / have been going
8. 'm / am making

Unit 9: Daily living
Lesson A: Listening
Exercise 1 page 102
1. broke into	4. robbed
2. stole	5. crime
3. robber	

Exercise 2 page 102
1. b	2. d	3. b	4. d

Exercise 3 page 103
1. break into	4. got into
2. robber	5. stole
3. came over	

Exercise 4 page 103
1. robbed	4. came over
2. broke into	5. crimes
3. mess	

Exercise 5 page 103
The robbers ran away because the car
didn't have any gas in it.

Lesson B: Past continuous
Exercise 1 page 104
1. was eating	4. were cleaning
2. was babysitting	5. was reading
3. were visiting	

Exercise 2 page 104
1. was knitting, was watching
2. was studying, was talking
3. was sleeping, was driving

Exercise 3 page 105
1. No, she wasn't.	3. Yes, they were.
2. Yes, they were.	4. No, he wasn't.

Exercise 4 page 105
1A. What was Anna doing at 9:00 a.m.?
1B. She was eating breakfast.
2A. What was Fareed doing at 2:00 p.m.?
2B. He was reading a book.
3A. What was Pete doing at 9:00 a.m.?
3B. He was painting the bedroom.
4A. What were Anna and Pete doing at
   2:00 p.m.?
4B. They were studying English.

Lesson C: Past continuous and
simple past
Exercise 1 page 106
1. We were jogging in the park when it
   started to rain.
2. I ran out of gas while I was driving to
   work.
3. Seema was having lunch with a friend
   when someone stole her car.
4. When the fire started, I was making
   cookies in the kitchen.
5. While the neighbors were attending a
   meeting, someone called the police.
6. Fatima was talking on the phone when
   her husband came home.

Exercise 2 page 106
1. was working	4. was driving
2. heard	5. hit
3. were talking	6. fell

Exercise 3 page 107
1. While we were eating lunch, the lights
   went out.
2. Ellen was sleeping when the fire alarm
   went off in her home.
3. When we got a parking ticket, we were
   shopping at the mall.
4. While Francisco was jogging, it started
   to rain.
5. While I was cooking dinner, my husband
   attended a meeting.
6. Julio and Tia were working in the
   garden when Julio fell off the ladder.

Exercise 4 page 107
1. While Chang was watching TV, the fire
   alarm went off.
2. When the lights went out, we were
   visiting our neighbors.
3. I was baking a cake when the
   earthquake started.
4. We were eating dinner when a thief
   stole my purse.
5. It began to rain while Fernando and
   Luis were painting the house.
6. We were driving in a bad storm when a
   tree fell on our car.
7. While Maria was taking a grammar
   test, Yan did her homework.

Lesson D: Reading
Exercise 1 page 108
1. d 2. c 3. b 4. d

Exercise 2 page 109
1. in 2006; A year later
  1B. In 2011.
2. in August; Two months later
  2B. In October.
3. In July; For the next three months
  3B. In October.
4. At 6:00 p.m.; Four minutes later
  4B. At 6:04 p.m.

Exercise 3 page 109
1. b, a 4. a, b
2. b, a 5. b, a
3. a, b

Lesson E: Writing
Exercise 1 page 110
1. The story is about a car accident.
2. The accident happened one evening last week.
3. The accident happened in the writer's neighborhood.
4. He was driving home from work.
5. A cat ran across the street, the writer turned the car, and then he hit a fire hydrant.
6. The writer told his wife he was going to be late.

Exercise 2 page 111
1. b 4. b 6. a
2. a 5. b 7. b
3. a

Exercise 3 page 111
Answer may vary.

Lesson F: Another view
Exercise 1 page 112
1. A 2. D 3. C 4. D 5. B 6. C

Exercise 2 page 113
1. N 5. OE
2. N 6. NF
3. NF 7. OE
4. NF 8. N

Exercise 3 page 113
1. Greg is taking a class at the garden center
2. 's / is taking some vegetables to the county fair
3. he is working in his garden
4. Nicole is trying to find a job as a salesperson
5. she's / is filling out a job application
6. she's / is going to a department store for an interview
7. Hamoud is collecting food for a family that lost their home in a flood.
8. he's / is taking the food to the family
9. he's / is calling some friends to ask them to give food

Unit 10: Free time
Lesson A: Listening
Exercise 1 page 114
1. days off 4. books
2. discounts 5. tax
3. round-trip 6. reserve

Exercise 2 page 114
By plane: $95.00, $269.00, $364.00
By train: $175.00, $134.50, $309.50
It is cheaper for Fabiola to travel by train.

Exercise 3 page 115
1. d 2. c 3. b 4. a

Exercise 4 page 115
1. Room rates are high in the summer.
2. You can get a discount if you book ahead.
3. You can reserve your hotel room online.
4. Sam has three days off.

Exercise 5 page 115
1. $638.00
2. $301.00

Exercise 6 page 115
1. NS 3. NS
2. S 4. S

Lesson B: Conditionals
Exercise 1 page 116
1. get, will go
2. will travel, aren't
3. is, will ride
4. visits, will stay
5. don't, won't

Exercise 2 page 116
1. If Jack's friends come over this afternoon, they'll play soccer.
2. If the weather is good, the Perez family will go hiking.
3. If Stacey has the day off, she will go shopping.
4. If it rains this weekend, Robert will read a book.

Exercise 3 page 117
1. have 5. comes
2. will visit 6. will go
3. will, do 7. doesn't come
4. don't have 8. will visit

Exercise 4 page 117
1A. What will Brian do if he has time off this summer?
1B. He will go swimming.
2A. What will Tam and Chen do if the weather is beautiful this weekend?
2B. They will work in the garden.
3A. What will Sara do if she gets some extra money for her birthday?
3B. She will go shopping.
4A. What will you do if you have a three-day weekend?
4B. I will go hiking.
5A. What will we do if the weather is bad?
5B. We will clean the house.

Lesson C: Future time clauses
Exercise 1 page 118
1. leaves 7. leaves
2. goes 8. leaves
3. will read 9. will buy
4. reads 10. will get
5. will find 11. will put
6. will choose

Exercise 2 page 118
1. Before Victor books a flight to Dallas, he will talk to a travel agent.
2. Victor will make a hotel reservation before he flies to Dallas.
3. After Victor cleans up the house, he will leave for the airport.
4. Victor will go through security after he checks in.
5. Before Victor gets on the plane, he will turn off his cell phone.

Exercise 3 page 119
1. a. Pedro will buy concert tickets before he invites Nick to the concert.
  b. Pedro will invite Nick to the concert after he buys concert tickets.
2. a. He will invite Nick to the concert before he makes dinner reservations.
  b. He will make dinner reservations after he invites Nick to the concert.
3. a. He will meet Nick after he finishes work.
  b. He will finish work before he meets Nick.
4. a. He will go to the concert after he eats dinner at a restaurant.
  b. He will eat dinner at a restaurant before he goes to the concert.

Exercise 4 page 119
1. What will you do before you go on your trip?
2. What will Trina do before she goes on vacation?
3. Where will they go after they leave New York?
4. What will Suzanna buy before she reads the newspaper?

Lesson D: Reading
Exercise 1 page 120
1. T 4. F 7. T
2. T 5. F 8. F
3. T 6. F

Exercise 2 page 121
1. The Statue of Liberty is the main topic of this article.
2. It's located in the middle of New York Harbor.
3. France gave the Statue of Liberty to the United States.
4. They gave it as a gift of friendship.
5. It's the day of America's independence from Britain.
6. There are 354 steps inside the statue.
7. You can see New York Harbor and the city's skyline from the crown.
8. You must take a ferry.

Exercise 3 page 121
1. a 4. a 7. b
2. a 5. b 8. a
3. b 6. a

Lesson E: Writing
Exercise 1 page 122
Answers may vary.

Exercise 2 page 123
Answer may vary.

Lesson F: Another view
Exercise 1 page 124
1. C 3. D 5. A
2. B 4. B 6. C

Exercise 2 page 125
1. B 4. A 7. C
2. B 5. C 8. B
3. A 6. A

Exercise 3 page 125
1. a 2. b 3. a 4. b 5. b 6. a

Illustration credits

Photography credits